THE TWELVE-TO-ONE HABIT

Noon-Time Recipes for the
Harried Cook
and the
Successful Hostess

by Ruth McPherson and
Marilyn Cassidy

ISBN 0-9690864-1-5

FOR MANY, LUNCH IS THE HARDEST MEAL TO PREPARE. IT IS USUALLY THE LIGHTEST REPAST OF THE DAY AND, THEREFORE, THE MENU IS LIMITED. SO WHEN MARILYN AND I DECIDED TO EMBARK ON ANOTHER CULINARY TRIP, LUNCH IN ITS MANY FORMS WAS THE UNANIMOUS CHOICE FOR A THEME - AND "THE TWELVE-TO-ONE HABIT" WAS BORN.

"BRUNCH" - THE FIRST SECTION - IS POPULAR WITH THE WEEK-END HOSTESS, ESPECIALLY IF THE GUESTS ARE LATE SLEEPERS. IT'S SO RELAXING TO BE ABLE TO DAWDLE OVER THE LAST CUP OF COFFEE, KNOWING THAT YOU DON'T HAVE TO RUSH TO GET THE BREAKFAST DISHES DONE SO THAT YOU CAN START PREPARING LUNCH.

THE WEEK-ENDS FLY BY AND BEFORE YOU STRETCHES ANOTHER WEEK OF LUNCH PAILS, BROWN BAGS AND FAMILY LUNCHES. WE HOPE THAT THE FOLLOWING RECIPES AND MENU SUGGESTIONS WILL HELP TO MAKE YOUR LUNCH PAILS AND BROWN BAGS MORE APPETIZING - AND YOUR HUSBAND AND CHILDREN APPRECIATE YOU MORE.

WHILE LUNCH IS USUALLY CONSIDERED A CASUAL, MID-DAY MEAL, IN HOUSEHOLDS WHERE THE MAN OF THE HOUSE IS ON THE FOUR-TO-TWELVE SHIFT, SOMETHING MORE SUBSTANTIAL IS CALLED FOR. FOR THESE FAMILIES WE HAVE INCLUDED HOT SANDWICHES, HAMBURG AND WEINER CASSEROLES, SOUPS AND EASY, FAMILY DESSERTS.

NOON-TIME ENTERTAINING IS FUN, BUT I FIND IT A REAL CHALLENGE TO PREPARE A LIGHT, APPETIZING MEAL THAT THE PREPARATION AND CLEAN-UP DOESN'T TIE ME TO THE STOVE AND KITCHEN FOR HOURS. IF YOU OFTEN HAVE YOUR NEIGHBOURS, THE BRIDGE CLUB OR THE LADIES FROM YOUR CHURCH CIRCLE IN FOR LUNCH, THE "LUNCH AT HOME - WITH STYLE" SECTION HAS BEEN PREPARED WITH EXPRESSLY YOU IN MIND.

WHEREAS SOME OF THE RECIPES IN THIS BOOK CAN'T BE PREPARED WITH THE EASE AND SPEED OF THOSE FROM "WITH A PINCH OF PINE CONES AND CHIPMUNKS," MOST OF THEM ARE UNCOMPLICATED AND EVERYTHING YOU NEED CAN BE OBTAINED AT YOUR LOCAL SUPERMARKET.

PERHAPS "THE TWELVE-TO-ONE HABIT" WILL BECOME "THE TWELVE-TO-ONE ADVENTURE." So read on - and benefit from our year of baking, cooking, tasting, testing - and gaining weight!

BRUNCH

THERE ARE MANY ADVANTAGES TO A BRUNCH. YOU CAN CATCH A FEW EXTRA HOURS' SLEEP AND STILL HAVE PLENTY OF TIME TO WHIP UP A DELECTABLE COMBINATION OF BREAKFAST AND LUNCH, SET THE TABLE WITH YOUR PRETTIEST PLACEMATS AND DISHES, GREET YOUR GUESTS AT THE DOOR LOOKING LIKE SOMEONE OUT OF A TV COMMERCIAL, THEN BASK IN THEIR PRAISE. BRUNCH IS THE EASIEST WAY TO ENTERTAIN. MANY OF THE DISHES CAN BE PREPARED AHEAD OF TIME AND THE CHOICE OF FOOD IS PRACTICALLY LIMITLESS.

MY FIRST BRUNCH EXPERIENCE WAS MANY YEARS AGO WHILE ATTENDING A WEDDING IN GRAND RAPIDS. OUR HOSTESS GAVE US A GLASS OF JUICE TO SUSTAIN US UNTIL ELEVEN, AND THEN WE WERE HUSTLED OVER TO THE GARDEN FUNCTION. AND WHAT A FEAST THAT WAS! OYSTERS, CHICKEN LIVERS, CHAMPAGNE - WAS IT BREAKFAST OR LUNCH? IT DIDN'T MATTER, BUT IT CERTAINLY WAS GLORIOUS.

WE THOUGHT IT MIGHT BE HELPFUL TO GIVE YOU COMPLETE BRUNCH MENUS, ALONG WITH THE RECIPES, OF COURSE. ALL THE RECIPES HAVE BEEN TRIED SEVERAL TIMES - THANKS TO NEIGHBOURS, FRIENDS AND RELATIVES FOR BEING SUCH UNDERSTANDING GUINEA PIGS. THE LITTLE GUY ACROSS THE STREET IS GROWING UP TO THINK OF SATURDAY AS THE DAY YOU DON'T GET ANY BREAKFAST, BUT YOU JUST GET BUNDLED UP AND CARRIED OVER TO "ROOFS" TO EAT A WHOLE

LOT OF FUNNY-LOOKING FOOD. HEREWITH, FOR ALL YOU GOURMETS-IN-TRAINING - AND FOR MATTHEW - THE RECIPES FOR THAT "FUNNY-LOOKING SATURDAY MORNING FOOD."

* * * *

I TRIED THE FOLLOWING BRUNCH OUT ON SOME OVERNIGHT GUESTS WHO DIDN'T GET UP VERY EARLY. IT HAS ENOUGH "BREAKFAST FOOD" IN IT THAT YOUR "CUSTOMERS" FEEL THEY ARE GETTING THE BEST MEAL OF THE DAY - AND YOU ARE SAVED THE BOTHER OF FUSSING OVER LUNCH.

GRAPEFRUIT ORANGE COMPOTE

MAKE-AHEAD SOUFFLÉS

ORANGE-GLAZED BACK BACON

BUBBLE BREAD

COFFEE - TEA

GRAPEFRUIT ORANGE COMPOTE

2 LARGE GRAPEFRUIT
4 LARGE ORANGES
1-1/2 CUPS SUGAR
3/4 CUP WATER

GRAPEFRUIT ORANGE COMPOTE - continued

PEEL ORANGES AND GRAPEFRUIT AND SECTION. REMOVE ALL THE WHITE FROM SOME OF THE ORANGE RIND AND CUT OUTER RIND INTO THIN SLICES TO MAKE 1/4 CUP. PUT INTO SAUCEPAN WITH WATER AND SUGAR, SIMMER, COVERED, ABOUT 20 MINUTES UNTIL RIND IS TENDER AND TRANSPARENT. UNCOVER AND CONTINUE COOKING UNTIL CONSISTENCY OF CORN SYRUP. POUR OVER FRUIT AND CHILL WELL..

MAKE-AHEAD SOUFFLÉS

THIS IS ONE OF MY FAVOURITE BRUNCH RECIPES. THESE SOUFFLÉS CAN BE MIXED UP SEVERAL WEEKS AHEAD AND KEPT IN THE FREEZER.

4 TABLESPOONS BUTTER (OR MARGARINE)

1/3 CUP ALL-PURPOSE FLOUR

3/4 TEASPOON SALT

1/8 TEASPOON PEPPER

1-1/2 CUPS MILK

2 CUPS SHREDDED PROCESS SWISS CHEESE

6 EGGS, SEPARATED

MELT BUTTER (OR MARGARINE) IN A MEDIUM SAUCEPAN. BLEND IN FLOUR, SALT AND PEPPER. ADD MILK. STIR CONSTANTLY OVER MEDIUM-HIGH HEAT UNTIL MIXTURE THICKENS AND BUBBLES. REMOVE FROM HEAT AND STIR IN CHEESE UNTIL MELTED. IN A LARGE BOWL, BEAT EGG WHITES WITH ELECTRIC MIXER ON HIGH

MAKE-AHEAD SOUFFLÉS - continued

SPEED UNTIL STIFF PEAKS FORM. IN A MEDIUM BOWL, BEAT EGG YOLKS WITH ELECTRIC MIXER ON HIGH SPEED UNTIL THICKENED AND LEMON-COLOURED - ABOUT 5 MINUTES. STIR CHEESE MIXTURE SLOWLY INTO EGG YOLKS. GRADUALLY POUR YOLK MIXTURE OVER EGG WHITES AND GENTLY FOLD TOGETHER. POUR MIXTURE INTO TEN 6-OUNCE CUSTARD CUPS OR SOUFFLÉ CUPS. COVER SOUFFLÉS WITH FOIL AND PLACE IN A 13" x 9" BAKING PAN AND A 9" SQUARE BAKING PAN. FREEZE SOUFFLÉS UNTIL 1-1/4 HOURS BEFORE SERVING TIME. BEFORE REMOVING SOUFFLÉS FROM FREEZER, PREHEAT OVEN TO 300 DEG. REMOVE SOUFFLÉS FROM FREEZER AND POUR HOT WATER 1/2" DEEP INTO BAKING PANS. BAKE FOR 1-1/4 HOURS OR UNTIL A KNIFE INSERTED IN CENTER COMES OUT CLEAN. SERVE AT ONCE. MAKES 5 OR 6 SERVINGS.

ORANGE-GLAZED BACK BACON

1 - 3-LB. PIECE BACK BACON
1/2 CUP BROWN SUGAR, FIRMLY PACKED
1 TABLESPOON ALL-PURPOSE FLOUR
1 TEASPOON DRY MUSTARD
1/2 TEASPOON GRATED ORANGE PEEL
1/4 TEASPOON GROUND CINNAMON
1/4 TEASPOON GROUND ALLSPICE
2 TABLESPOONS ORANGE JUICE
1 ORANGE, THINLY SLICED

PREHEAT OVEN TO 350 DEGREES F. PLACE BACON IN AN 11" x 7" BAKING DISH. BAKE FOR 1 HOUR AND 30 MINUTES,

ORANGE-GLAZED BACK BACON - continued

OR UNTIL ALMOST TENDER. IN A SMALL BOWL, MIX BROWN SUGAR, FLOUR, DRY MUSTARD, ORANGE PEEL, CINNAMON AND ALLSPICE. STIR IN ORANGE JUICE. SPOON HALF THE ORANGE GLAZE OVER THE BACON AND TOP WITH ORANGE SLICES. CONTINUE BAKING UNTIL COMPLETELY TENDER (ABOUT 30 MINUTES), BASTING WITH REMAINING GLAZE SEVERAL TIMES. CUT IN THICK SLICES. MAKES 8 TO 10 SERVINGS, OR GREAT FOR SANDWICHES FROM THE LEFTOVERS.

BUBBLE BREAD

THIS IS AMBROSIA! MARILYN MADE THIS ONE AFTERNOON AND SERVED IT HOT, FRESH FROM THE OVEN, FOR SUPPER. WE COULDN'T STOP EATING IT, AND THREE OF US FINISHED OFF THE WHOLE LOAF AT ONE SITTING. YOU WILL TOO.

BASIC SWEET DOUGH:

1/2 CUP MILK	1/4 CUP SUGAR + 1 TEASPOON
4 TABLESPOONS MARGARINE	1/2 TEASPOON SALT
1/4 CUP LUKEWARM WATER	1 PACKAGE DRY YEAST
ABOUT 2-1/4 CUPS ALL-PURPOSE FLOUR	1 EGG

DISSOLVE 1 TEASPOON SUGAR IN 1/4 CUP LUKEWARM WATER. ADD YEAST AND LET STAND ABOUT 10 MINUTES.

BASIC SWEET DOUGH for BUBBLE BREAD - continued

SCALD MILK - ADD MARGARINE, SUGAR AND SALT. COOL TO LUKEWARM. STIR DOWN DISSOLVED YEAST AND ADD TO COOLED MILK MIXTURE. ADD EGG AND 1/2 CUP FLOUR. BEAT AT HIGH SPEED 2 MINUTES. STIR IN ENOUGH OF REMAINING FLOUR TO MAKE MODERATELY STIFF DOUGH. (MAY TAKE MORE OR LESS, DEPENDING ON CONDITIONS). KNEAD 3 - 5 MINUTES UNTIL SMOOTH AND ELASTIC. PUT INTO GREASED BOWL AND ALLOW TO RISE 1 HOUR OR UNTIL DOUBLE. PUNCH DOWN, TURN OUT ONTO FLOURED BOARD AND LET REST, COVERED, FOR 10 MINUTES, BEFORE PROCEEDING WITH BUBBLE BREAD.

BUBBLE BREAD:

2/3 CUP GRANULATED SUGAR

1 TEASPOON GROUND CINNAMON

5 TABLESPOONS BUTTER OR MARGARINE, MELTED

1/2 CUP BROWN SUGAR, FIRMLY PACKED

2 TABLESPOONS LIGHT CORN SYRUP

2 TABLESPOONS BUTTER OR MARGARINE

1/4 TEASPOON MAPLE FLAVOURING

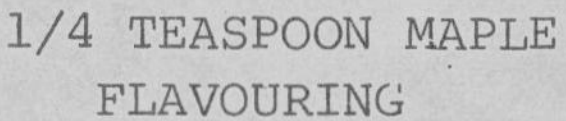

BUBBLE BREAD - continued

PREPARE BASIC SWEET DOUGH. GREASE A 9" TUBE PAN; SET ASIDE. SHAPE DOUGH INTO ABOUT THIRTY 1" BALLS. IN A PIE PLATE, MIX GRANULATED SUGAR AND CINNAMON. DIP BALLS INTO 5 TABLESPOONS MELTED BUTTER OR MARGARINE, THEN ROLL IN CINNAMON-SUGAR MIXTURE. ARRANGE BALLS IN LAYERS IN THE GREASED TUBE PAN. COVER AND LET RISE IN A WARM PLACE ABOUT 40 MINUTES OR UNTIL DOUBLED IN BULK. PREHEAT OVEN TO 375 DEGREES F. IN A SMALL SAUCEPAN, MELT 2 TABLESPOONS BUTTER OR MARGARINE. STIR IN BROWN SUGAR, CORN SYRUP, AND MAPLE FLAVORING. POUR BROWN SUGAR MIXTURE OVER RISEN DOUGH. BAKE FOR 35 MINUTES. BREAD IS DONE WHEN IT IS NO LONGER DOUGHY. TO BE SURE, YOU MAY HAVE TO PULL OFF A BUBBLE. COOL IN PAN 10 MINUTES. INVERT ONTO A PLATTER: REMOVE PAN. SERVE BREAD WARM. MAKES ONE RING. IT'S TOO GOOD - IT DOESN'T SERVE MANY!

THE TITLE OF A COOKBOOK I WAS GIVEN LAST YEAR - "I DON'T HAVE A MINUTE TO SPARE" - DESCRIBES MARILYN AND ME TO A "T". HERE'S AN EASY, SATISFYING BRUNCH MENU THAT WE THINK YOU WILL LIKE.

GLAZED BREAKFAST FRUITS

COMPANY BREAKFAST

BLUEBERRY-PINEAPPLE COFFEE CAKE

COFFEE

GLAZED BREAKFAST FRUIT

4 PEARS, HALVED
4 PEACHES, HALVED
6 APRICOTS, HALVED
1/4 CUP BROWN SUGAR
1/4 STICK MARGARINE

PLACE FRUIT IN SECTIONS IN SHALLOW BUTTERED BAKING DISH. SPRINKLE WITH BROWN SUGAR AND DOT WITH BUTTER. BAKE AT 450 DEGREES FOR 15 TO 20 MINUTES.

COMPANY BREAKFAST

I DON'T THINK THIS IS APPROPRIATELY NAMED. I'VE SERVED IT AT 11:00 A.M. TO BLUE-JEANED NEIGHBOURS, NIECES AND THEIR SNIFFLY-NOSED YOUNGSTERS AND TO FRIENDS I'VE LITERALLY HAULED IN OFF THE STREET TO BE "GUINEA PIGS." THEY'VE ALL LIKED IT. IF YOU EVER WANT AN HONEST OPINION ABOUT ANYTHING - CLOTHES, HOUSE DECORATING, HAIR-DOS OR FOOD - JUST ASK NIECES. THEY'LL TELL YOU!

1 POUND PORK SAUSAGES <u>or</u>
1 POUND BULK SAUSAGE MEAT
6 EGGS
2 CUPS MILK
1 TEASPOON SALT
1 TEASPOON DRY MUSTARD
4 SLICES BREAD - CUBED
1 CUP GRATED CHEDDAR CHEESE

COOK AND DRAIN THE SAUSAGES OR SAUSAGE MEAT. LAYER BREAD CUBES, SAUSAGE AND CHEESE IN THAT ORDER IN A 9 x 13 PAN. MIX EGGS, MILK, SALT AND MUSTARD AND POUR OVER TOP. BAKE FOR 45 MINUTES AT 350 DEGREES. SERVES 6.

MAY BE MADE NIGHT BEFORE AND REFRIGERATED UNBAKED.

BLUEBERRY-PINEAPPLE COFFEE CAKE

THIS IS A VERY MOIST COFFEE CAKE THAT GOES WELL WITH ANY MENU. LIKE A LOT OF CAKES THAT ARE SO SINFULLY GOOD, IT'S NOT FOR THE CALORIE CONSCIOUS.

1/3 CUP BUTTER OR MARGARINE, SOFTENED
1/3 CUP BROWN SUGAR (PACKED)
1/2 CUP FLAKED COCONUT
1 PACKAGE (13.5 OUNCES) WILD BLUEBERRY MUFFIN MIX
1 CAN (8-1/2 OUNCES) CRUSHED PINEAPPLE, WELL DRAINED

HEAT OVEN TO 400 DEGREES. GREASE 9 x 9 PAN. MIX BUTTER, SUGAR AND COCONUT; SET ASIDE.
PREPARE MUFFIN MIX AS DIRECTED ON PACKAGE AND FOLD IN CRUSHED PINEAPPLE. POUR INTO PAN. SPOON COCONUT MIXTURE EVENLY OVER BATTER. BAKE 25 TO 30 MINUTES OR UNTIL GOLDEN BROWN. THIS IS SUPPOSED TO MAKE 9 SERVINGS, BUT YOU SHOULD EXPECT TO SERVE SECONDS - EVERYONE WILL ASK FOR MORE!

THIS NEXT MENU IS FOR MAKING AN IMPRESSION. YOU COULD ALWAYS SERVE IT TO YOUR HUSBAND, BUT HE MIGHT THINK YOU'RE UP TO NO GOOD! WE GIVE YOU THE FOLLOWING MOUTH-WATERING RECIPES; THE GUEST LIST IS UP TO YOU.

MARINATED ORANGES

SKILLET APPLE PANCAKES

SAUSAGES

CINNAMON TWIST COFFEE CAKE

MARINATED ORANGES

2 TEASPOONS SHREDDED ORANGE PEEL
1 TABLESPOON SUGAR
1 TABLESPOON ORANGE JUICE
1 TABLESPOON GRAND MARNIER (OR ANY FRUIT LIQUEUR)
2 LARGE, SEEDLESS ORANGES (RIND AND PITH REMOVED)
CUT INTO 1/2" SLICES

GENTLY MIX PEEL, SUGAR, ORANGE JUICE AND LIQUEUR. POUR OVER ORANGE SLICES, COVER TIGHTLY AND CHILL AT LEAST 1 HOUR, PREFERABLY OVERNIGHT. LET STAND AT ROOM TEMPERATURE AT LEAST 20 MINUTES BEFORE SERVING. ARRANGE IN SHALLOW DISH, SPOONING SAUCE OVER TOP. DOUBLE FOR 4 SERVINGS.

SKILLET APPLE PANCAKE

3 EGGS
1/2 CUP MILK
1/3 CUP FLOUR
1/4 TEASPOON SALT
2 GREEN APPLES
2 TABLESPOONS LEMON JUICE
1/4 CUP BUTTER
1/4 CUP SUGAR
1/4 TEASPOON CINNAMON
LEMON JUICE

MIX EGGS, MILK, FLOUR AND SALT IN A BLENDER, OR MIX WITH ELECTRIC BEATER, UNTIL SMOOTH. LET THE BATTER STAND AT ROOM TEMPERATURE 1 HOUR. CORE, PEEL AND THINLY SLICE APPLES AND SPRINKLE WITH 2 TABLESPOONS OF LEMON JUICE. IN A HEAVY 12" SKILLET, MELT 2 TABLESPOONS BUTTER; POUR IN THE BATTER. COVER WITH APPLE SLICES AND BAKE AT 375 DEGREES FOR 10 TO 15 MINUTES. PLACE THE PANCAKE IN A SERVING DISH AND SPREAD WITH 2 TABLESPOONS SOFTENED BUTTER.
COMBINE SUGAR AND CINNAMON AND SPRINKLE OVER APPLES. SPRINKLE LEMON JUICE OVER TO TASTE. SERVES 4.

ENJOY! THIS IS SPECIAL.

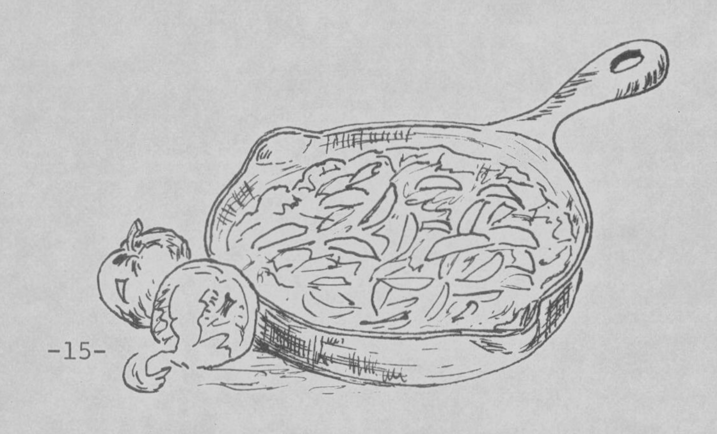

CINNAMON TWIST COFFEE CAKE

THIS RECIPE USES THE SAME BASIC SWEET DOUGH RECIPE AS THE BUBBLE BREAD ON PAGE 8 AND IS JUST SUPER.

- BASIC SWEET DOUGH (PAGE 8)
- 3 TABLESPOONS BUTTER OR MARGARINE, MELTED
- 1/2 CUP BROWN SUGAR, FIRMLY PACKED
- 1-1/2 TEASPOONS GROUND CINNAMON
- 1/2 CUP SEEDLESS RAISINS
- POWDERED SUGAR GLAZE

POWDERED SUGAR GLAZE:

- 1 CUP POWDERED SUGAR
- 2 TABLESPOONS MILK
- 1/4 TEASPOON VANILLA EXTRACT

PREPARE BASIC SWEET DOUGH. GREASE A 9" SQUARE PAN; SET ASIDE. ON A LIGHTLY FLOURED BOARD, ROLL OUT DOUGH TO A 12" SQUARE. BRUSH LIGHTLY WITH MELTED BUTTER OR MARGARINE. IN A SMALL BOWL, MIX BROWN SUGAR AND CINNAMON. SPRINKLE A STRIP DOWN CENTER THIRD OF SQUARE WITH HALF THE CINNAMON-SUGAR MIXTURE, THEN SPRINKLE WITH HALF THE RAISINS. FOLD ONE-THIRD OF DOUGH OVER CENTER THIRD. SPRINKLE THE DOUBLE LAYER OF DOUGH WITH REMAINING CINNAMON-SUGAR MIXTURE AND RAISINS. FOLD REMAINING THIRD OF DOUGH OVER; SEAL

CINNAMON TWIST COFFEE CAKE - continued

EDGE. CUT CROSSWISE INTO TWELVE 1" STRIPS. HOLDING THE ENDS OF EACH STRIP, TWIST TIGHTLY IN OPPOSITE DIRECTIONS. ARRANGE 2 ROWS OF 6 TWISTS EACH IN THE GREASED PAN AND COVER. LET RISE IN A WARM PLACE ABOUT 30 MINUTES OR UNTIL DOUBLED IN BULK. PREHEAT OVEN TO 375 DEGREES F. BAKE 25 TO 30 MINUTES OR UNTIL GOLDEN BROWN. COOL IN PAN 10 MINUTES. WHILE COOLING, PREPARE POWDERED SUGAR GLAZE -

MIX POWDERED SUGAR, MILK AND VANILLA. BEAT UNTIL SMOOTH. PLACE COFFEE CAKE ON PLATE AND DRIZZLE POWDERED SUGAR GLAZE OVER IT. BE PREPARED TO RECEIVE LOTS OF BOUQUETS!

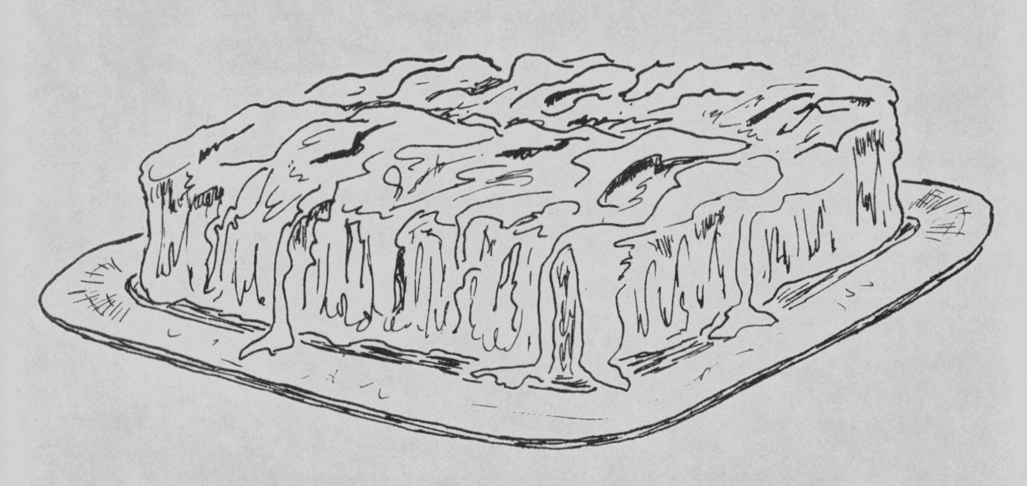

A GALA BRUNCH

BRUNCH IS A FUN WAY TO ENTERTAIN AT ANY TIME, BUT ESPECIALLY SO ON SPECIAL OCCASIONS - BOXING DAY, NEW YEAR'S DAY (WHEN EVERYONE'S TIRED OF BIG, TURKEY DINNERS), GREY CUP DAY - OR A "BEAT THE MID-WINTER BLUES" SATURDAY BRUNCH. I DON'T KNOW ABOUT YOU, BUT I THINK BRIDAL SHOWERS ARE SOMETIMES A REAL BORE. WHY NOT GIVE A BRUNCH INSTEAD? AND FOR A DIFFERENT TWIST, INSTEAD OF THE CONVENTIONAL COFFEE MUGS, TEA TOWELS, CASSEROLES, VASES, ETC., THE GUESTS COULD BE ASKED TO BRING THEIR FAVOURITE RECIPE AND ALONG WITH IT, THE UTENSIL IT'S MADE IN OR SERVED ON.

CRANBERRY PUNCH

FRUIT KABOB AND DIP

PEANUT BUTTER FINGERS

CHICKEN SQUARES WITH MUSHROOM SAUCE

ASSORTED CHEESE BOARD WITH CLUSTERS OF GRAPES AND CRACKERS

CINNAMON BREAKFAST PUFFS

COFFEE - TEA

CRANBERRY PUNCH

1 - 40-OUNCE BOTTLE CRANBERRY COCKTAIL, CHILLED

1-1/4 CUPS WHITE WINE, CHILLED

1-1/4 CUPS CLUB SODA CHILLED

MIX TOGETHER AND SERVE. MAKES 12 DRINKS

FRUIT KABOBS WITH DIP

1 - 8-OUNCE PACKAGE CREAM CHEESE

1 - 7-OUNCE JAR MARSHMALLOW CREAM

PINCH OF GINGER

1 TABLESPOON ORANGE RIND

CHUNKY FRUITS - STRAWBERRIES, PINEAPPLE, BANANA, APPLE, ORANGES, CANTALOUPE, ETC.

COMBINE FIRST 4 INGREDIENTS. SKEWER FRUITS ON COCKTAIL MUDDLERS AND ARRANGE AROUND DIP ON ATTRACTIVE PLATTER.

PEANUT BUTTER FINGERS

YOUR GUESTS WILL NEVER GUESS WHAT'S IN THESE SIMPLE CANAPÉS. EVERYONE WILL THINK THEY'RE TERRIFIC, SO YOU MIGHT AS WELL DOUBLE THE RECIPE TO BEGIN WITH.

6 SLICES BREAD, THINLY SLICED
1/2 CUP PEANUT BUTTER
1/2 CUP BUTTER
FINE BREAD CRUMBS

REMOVE CRUSTS FROM BREAD AND CUT INTO 1/2" THIN FINGERS. PLACE IN A SLOW (250 DEGREES) OVEN AND TOAST UNTIL BROWN. SHAKE THEM OCCASIONALLY TO TOAST EVENLY. IN A DOUBLE BOILER, MELT BUTTER AND PEANUT BUTTER TOGETHER. WHEN DONE, DIP FINGERS IN PEANUT BUTTER MIXTURE AND PLACE ON WAX PAPER UNTIL COOL. SHAKE IN BREAD CRUMBS. SERVE OR STORE IN REFRIGERATOR IN TIGHTLY SEALED CONTAINER. THESE WILL KEEP FOR AGES, BUT YOU WON'T HAVE ANY LEFT OVER AFTER SERVING THEM.

CHICKEN SQUARES WITH MUSHROOM SAUCE

THIS RECIPE GETS RAVE REVIEWS WHENEVER IT IS SERVED. IF YOU DON'T BELIEVE ME, TRY IT OUT ON THE FAMILY AND WATCH THEM ASK FOR SECONDS.

3 CUPS CHICKEN (OR TURKEY) COOKED AND DICED

1 CUP COOKED RICE

2 CUPS SOFT BREAD CRUMBS

1/3 CUP DICED CELERY

1/2 CUP CHOPPED PIMENTO

4 BEATEN EGGS

2 TEASPOONS SALT

1/2 TEASPOON POULTRY SEASONING

2 CUPS CHICKEN BROTH (MAY DISSOLVE 2 CHICKEN BOUILLON CUBES IN 2 CUPS HOT WATER, THEN COOL)

COMBINE CHICKEN, RICE, BREAD CRUMBS, CELERY AND PIMENTO. BEAT EGGS AND ADD - SALT, POULTRY SEASONING AND BROTH. MIX THOROUGHLY, AND STIR INTO CHICKEN MIXTURE. BAKE IN GREASED 9 x 9 DISH AT 350 DEGREES FOR 55 MINUTES. CUT IN SQUARES AND SERVE WITH MUSHROOM SAUCE.

SAUCE: 1/3 CUP MILK
1 CAN OF CREAM OF MUSHROOM SOUP

BEAT THE MILK AND SOUP THOROUGHLY, HEAT AND POUR OVER SQUARES.

MAKES 9 SERVINGS.

CINNAMON BREAKFAST PUFFS

THESE ARE THE CAT'S PYJAMAS (BOY, AM I DATING MYSELF!) IF YOU SERVE THEM AT A PRE-WEDDING PARTY, THE BRIDE MAY HAVE TO LET THE SEAMS OUT ON HER WEDDING DRESS!

- 1/3 CUP SHORTENING
- 1/2 CUP SUGAR
- 1 EGG
- 1-1/2 CUPS SIFTED, ALL-PURPOSE FLOUR
- 1-1/2 TEASPOONS BAKING POWDER
- 1/2 TEASPOON SALT
- 1/4 TEASPOON NUTMEG
- 1/2 CUP MILK
- 1/2 CUP SUGAR
- 1 TEASPOON CINNAMON
- 1/2 CUP BUTTER OR MARGARINE, MELTED

HEAT OVEN TO 350 DEGREES. GREASE 12 MEDIUM MUFFIN CUPS (2-3/4" IN DIA.). MIX THOROUGHLY SHORTENING, 1/2 CUP SUGAR AND THE EGG. STIR IN FLOUR, BAKING POWDER, SALT AND NUTMEG ALTERNATELY WITH MILK. FILL MUFFIN CUPS 2/3 FULL. BAKE 20 TO 25 MINUTES.
MIX 1/2 CUP SUGAR AND THE CINNAMON. IMMEDIATELY AFTER BAKING, ROLL PUFFS IN MELTED BUTTER, THEN IN CINNAMON-SUGAR MIXTURE. SERVE HOT.

ADDITIONAL FAVOURITE RECIPES

ADDITIONAL FAVOURITE RECIPES

HERCULES
5
MADE IN CANADA
BROWN
Bagging
M CASSIDY

THIS SECTION IS THE MAIN REASON FOR A 12 - 1 COOKBOOK. I'M AN OCCASIONAL BROWN-BAGGER, AND I DO LACK ENTHUSIASM OR INSPIRATION WHEN I'M RUSHING AROUND IN THE MORNING, OR THE NIGHT BEFORE, TRYING TO FIND SOMETHING APPETIZING AND LOW-CALORIED TO TAKE TO WORK. THE ONLY ALTERNATIVE IS TO "EAT OUT." I OCCASIONALLY SUCCUMB TO THE BLANDISHMENTS OF THE LOCAL EATERIES, FAST-SERVE OR SOPHISTICATED, BUT THIS IS MURDER ON THE FIGURE, NOT TO MENTION THE BUDGET!

THE EFFICIENT LUNCH CARRIER IS ONE WHO MAKES SANDWICH FILLERS AHEAD OF TIME, BAKES HER OWN COOKIES AND CAKES AND COUNTS CALORIES ALONG WITH THE PENNIES. IT WORKS! I HAVE HARD-COOKED AND CHOPPED EGGS, MINCED ONIONS AND CELERY, THIN SLICED LEFT-OVER HAM, ROAST, TURKEY, CHICKEN, ETC., AND PUT THEM IN LITTLE PLASTIC BAGS, ALL READY TO SANDWICH BETWEEN A ROLL OR BREAD; BAKED COOKIES, LOAVES, CAKES. LIKE THE BOY SCOUTS, I'M PREPARED!

WE START THIS SECTION WITH THE STANDARD LUNCH CARRIER'S FARE - S A N D W I C H E S. A SANDWICH CAN BE VERY VERSATILE; IT CAN BE A LOWLY "CHOPPED-EGG-OR-BOLOGNA-BETWEEN-TWO-SLICES-OF-BREAD" VARIETY OR IT CAN BE A MANY-SPLENDORED THING MADE OF LOBSTER, CRAB MEAT, BARBECUED BEEF, ETC. WE LIKE THE FOLLOWING IN-BETWEEN VARIETIES. WE HOPE YOU DO TOO.

MIX APPLE SLICES WITH DEVILLED HAM TO USE AS FILLING BETWEEN TWO VERY THIN SLICES OF BREAD.

APPLES GO EVERYWHERE! TRY SLICES OF THEM WITH PEANUT BUTTER - BETWEEN BREAD, OF COURSE.

CREAM CHEESE MIXED WITH CHOPPED DATES AND A LITTLE BIT OF ORANGE RIND MAKES A DELICIOUS SPREAD ON BROWN BREAD.

CHOPPED HAM AND CHOPPED WALNUTS, HELD TOGETHER WITH A LITTLE MAYONNAISE ARE DELICIOUS AS A SANDWICH FILLING!

SO IS CHEESE WHIZ AND FRESH, CHOPPED PARSLEY.

THE APPLE HAS COMPETITION! THERE'S ALL KINDS OF WAYS TO DRESS UP A PEANUT BUTTER SANDWICH, AND NOT ONLY CHILDREN LIKE IT! IT CAN BE MIXED WITH RAISINS - NUTS - CRUMBLED BACON (A REAL WINNER) - OR DRAINED, CRUSHED PINEAPPLE.

CHEESE IS A UNIVERSAL LUNCH FAVOURITE, WHETHER IT BE IN A SOUFFLÉ, A QUICHE, SOUP - OR IN A SANDWICH. EVER TRY IT WITH STRAWBERRY JAM? OR CHEESE SLICES WITH SLICED PINEAPPLE?

THE FOLLOWING RECIPE OF MARILYN'S IS A GOOD KEEPER:

CHEESE SANDWICH SPREAD

1/2 POUND VELVEETA CHEESE
1/2 CUP CHOPPED GREEN PEPPER
1 PIMENTO
1/2 SMALL ONION, GRATED
1/4 CUP CHILI SAUCE
1/2 TEASPOON SALT
PEPPER

COMBINE ALL INGREDIENTS OVER DOUBLE BOILER. HEAT UNTIL CHEESE IS MELTED, STIRRING OCCASIONALLY. MIX WELL. REMOVE FROM HEAT AND PUT INTO COVERED REFRIGERATOR CONTAINER. KEEPS WELL REFRIGERATED.

HOT DOGS IN A THERMOS

WE SUGGESTED THIS IN "WITH A PINCH OF PINE CONES AND CHIPMUNKS." IN THAT BOOK IT WAS RECOMMENDED FOR CHILDREN TO TAKE ON PICNICS. BUT EVERYONE LIKES HOT DOGS AND THEY'RE "AT HOME" IN THE MILL, THE LUNCH ROOM AT THE OFFICE OR IN THE PARK ON A SUNNY, SUMMER LUNCH-HOUR.

WEINERS - HOT DOG BUNS - MUSTARD - KETCHUP

HEAT WEINERS AND PUT THEM IN A WIDE-MOUTH THERMOS THAT HAS BEEN FILLED WITH HOT WATER. PACK BUNS, SPREAD WITH MUSTARD AND/OR KETCHUP, AND AT LUNCHTIME ALL YOU HAVE TO DO IS POUR THE WATER OUT OF THE THERMOS AND PUT THE WEINERS IN THE BUNS. IF YOU HAVE TO GO OUT AND BUY A WIDE-MOUTH THERMOS, USE IT THE NEXT TIME FOR SOUP OR CHILE.

HERE'S MY FAVOURITE BROWN-BAGGER'S LUNCH -

RAW ZUCCHINI, CAULIFLOWER, RADISHES, PEPPERS, CARROTS; MY FAVOURITE DRESSING IN A SEALED, PLASTIC CUP;
A COUPLE OF WEDGES OF FOIL-WRAPPED CHEESE
A HARD-COOKED EGG
A BRAN MUFFIN
FRESH FRUIT

A LUNCH LIKE THIS HELPS YOU FIGHT THE BATTLE OF THE BULGE!

DURING THE SUMMER I LIKE TO MIX ALL THE FRUITS OF THE SEASON TOGETHER IN A SEAL-AND-STORE CONTAINER FOR A LOW CALORIE, REFRESHING LUNCH. ADD TO THIS A SLICE OF RAISIN BREAD SPREAD WITH CREAM CHEESE AND YOU HAVE A NUTRITIOUS MEAL AS WELL.

WHEN SENDING ICED CAKE IN A LUNCH PAIL, SPLIT THE CAKE IN HALF AND PLACE THE BOTTOM HALF ON TOP OF THE ICING.

SOUP IS A POPULAR LUNCH-TIME ITEM AND, WITH APOLOGIES TO MESSRS. HEINZ AND CAMPBELL, WHAT COULD BE BETTER THAN A CUP OF THICK, SUCCULENT, HOME-MADE SOUP!

HAMBURGER SOUP

1 POUND LEAN GROUND BEEF

3 MEDIUM ONIONS, SLICED

1 - 19-OUNCE CAN TOMATOES

2 TEASPOONS SALT, OR TO TASTE

1/4 TEASPOON PEPPER

6 CUPS BEEF BROTH OR WATER (IF POSSIBLE, WATER SAVED FROM VEGETABLE COOKING)

2 BEEF BOUILLON CUBES - IF WATER IS USED

1 CUP SLICED CARROTS

1 CUP SLICED CELERY

1 CUP DICED POTATOES

MUSHROOMS - OPTIONAL

BROWN BEEF, BREAKING UP AS IT IS BROWNING. ADD ONIONS, TOMATOES, SALT, PEPPER, BEEF BROTH (OR WATER AND BOUILLON CUBES). SIMMER 30 MINUTES. STIR IN VEGETABLES AND SIMMER, COVERED, FOR 45 MINUTES OR UNTIL VEGETABLES ARE TENDER.

MAKES ABOUT 8 SERVINGS.

I LIKE GOING OUT FOR LUNCH WITH THE GIRLS FROM THE OFFICE, BUT THEY SAY "NO THANK YOU" TO DESSERT. THAT I DON'T LIKE. THE WAITRESS GRABS THE MENU OUT OF MY HAND AND IS OFF WITH IT BEFORE I EVEN HAVE A CHANCE TO SUGGEST THAT A SMALL WEDGE OF BANANA CREAM PIE ---------------. OH WELL, THERE'S ALWAYS THE COFFEE CART AT 3 O'CLOCK! BUT WHEN BROWN-BAGGING IT, I THROW CAUTION TO THE WIND AND PACK SOMETHING HOME-MADE AND CALORIE-LADEN. I WAS ONCE LIKE THAT SLIM, YOUNG THING MUNCHING CELERY AND CARROT STICKS OVER IN THE CORNER!

THE FOLLOWING ALL PACK WELL AND ARE EASY TO MAKE:

BROWN BAGGER'S CAKE

- 1 CUP SUGAR
- 1 CUP SALAD OIL
- 4 EGGS
- 1 CUP ALL-PURPOSE FLOUR
- 1 CUP WHOLE WHEAT FLOUR
- 1-1/2 TEASPOONS BAKING SODA
- 1 TEASPOON SALT
- 2 TEASPOONS CINNAMON
- 2 CUPS GRATED RAW CARROTS
- 1-1/2 CUPS GRATED APPLES
- 1 CUP RAISINS
- 1/2 CUP CHOPPED WALNUTS (OPTIONAL)

BLEND TOGETHER SUGAR, OIL AND EGGS. BEAT 'TIL SLIGHTLY THICKENED. SIFT TOGETHER DRY INGREDIENTS AND COMBINE WITH EGG MIXTURE. ADD CARROT, APPLE, RAISINS AND NUTS AND BLEND. BAKE IN GREASED AND FLOURED 9 x 13 PAN AT 350 DEGREES FOR 35 TO 40 MINUTES.

BROWN BAGGER'S CAKE - continued

CREAM CHEESE FROSTING:

1 - 4-OUNCE PACKAGE CREAM CHEESE, SOFTENED

1/4 CUP BUTTER

1 CUP ICING SUGAR (MAY REQUIRE MORE)

1/2 TEASPOON VANILLA

BEAT CHEESE AND BUTTER UNTIL FLUFFY. BEAT IN ICING SUGAR AND VANILLA UNTIL WELL COMBINED.

RICE KRISPIE COOKIES

I LOVE COOKIES THAT YOU CAN KEEP IN THE FREEZER UNTIL IT'S TIME TO BAKE THEM. HERE'S A GOOD COOKIE WITH SNAP, CRACKLE AND POP -

1 CUP SUGAR

1 CUP BROWN SUGAR

1 CUP SOFTENED BUTTER
(OR MARGARINE)

1 TEASPOON VANILLA

PINCH OF SALT

2 EGGS

1 CUP QUICK OATMEAL

2 CUPS FLOUR

1 TEASPOON BAKING SODA

2 CUPS RICE KRISPIES

MIX ALL INGREDIENTS WELL, SPOONING IN RICE KRISPIES LAST. SHAPE INTO LONG, THIN ROLLS AND FREEZE (DOUBLE WRAPPED, IF TO BE KEPT FOR A LONG PERIOD OF TIME). SLICE VERY THIN WHEN FROZEN, AND PLACE ON UNGREASED COOKIE SHEET. BAKE AT 375 DEG. FOR 8 TO 10 MINUTES UNTIL LIGHTLY BROWNED. KEEP THE DOUGH FROZEN AND SLICE OFF WHAT YOU NEED. MEANS HAVING FRESH, HOT COOKIES ON THE TABLE IN 10 MINUTES.

ICEBOX GINGER COOKIES

1 CUP BUTTER
1 CUP SUGAR
1/2 CUP MOLASSES
1 TEASPOON BAKING SODA
2 TEASPOONS GINGER
1 TEASPOON VANILLA
1 TEASPOON SALT
2-1/2 CUPS SIFTED FLOUR

MELT THE BUTTER, POUR IT OVER THE SUGAR AND ADD THE MOLASSES. ADD THE REST OF THE INGREDIENTS AND MIX WELL. FORM INTO TWO ROLLS AND WRAP IN WAXED PAPER. CHILL WELL IN REFRIGERATOR. SLICE THIN AND BAKE AT 400 DEGREES F. FOR 8 - 9 MINUTES, ON WELL-GREASED COOKIE SHEET. OR YOU CAN FREEZE THEM AND BAKE THEM WHEN YOU NEED THEM.

MY KIND OF COOKIES!

PATCHWORK COOKIES

MIX TOGETHER:

3/4 CUP MARGARINE
1/2 CUP SUGAR
1-2/3 CUPS CAKE FLOUR (SCANT)
1 TEASPOON BAKING POWDER
4 TABLESPOONS COCOA
3 CUPS CORNFLAKES
1/2 TEASPOON SALT

DROP BY TEASPOONFUL ON COOKIE SHEET; BAKE AT 375 DEGREES FOR 15 - 20 MINUTES. IF DESIRED, FROST WITH CHOCOLATE ICING.

POPPY SEED CAKE

1 PACKAGE YELLOW CAKE MIX

1 PACKAGE INSTANT TOASTED COCONUT PUDDING MIX

1/4 CUP POPPY SEEDS

4 EGGS

1/2 CUP SALAD OIL

1 CUP HOT WATER

BEAT ALL TOGETHER 'TIL MIXED. POUR INTO 2 LARGE (5 x 9) BREAD TINS. HAVE TINS WELL GREASED AND LIGHTLY FLOURED. BAKE AT 350 DEGREES FOR 40 TO 50 MINUTES (UNTIL A PIECE OF THE BROOM COMES OUT CLEAN).
HAVE ALSO USED LEMON CAKE MIX AND ORANGE CAKE MIX.
IF YOU CAN'T FIND TOASTED COCONUT PUDDING MIX IN OUR STORES (I CAN'T), JUST USE A VANILLA PUDDING MIX AND ADD A BIT OF TOASTED COCONUT.

MEN LIKE THIS. IT'S VERY PLAIN - NOT ALL GUSSIED UP WITH ICING, WHIPPED CREAM, ETC.

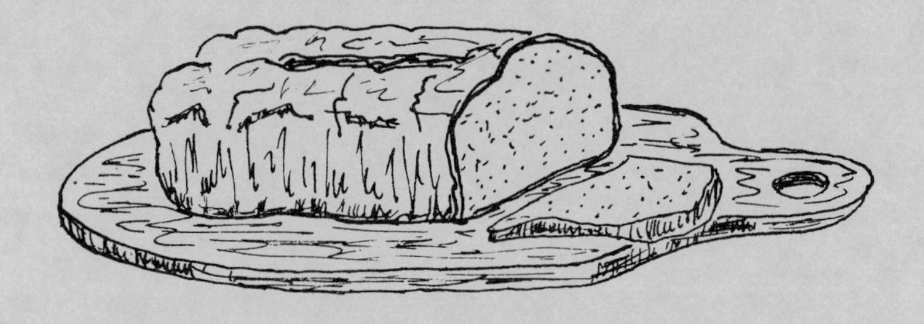

BANANA BRAN BREAD

1-1/2 CUPS SIFTED ALL-PURPOSE FLOUR

2 TEASPOONS BAKING POWDER

1/2 TEASPOON BAKING SODA

1/2 TEASPOON SALT

1/2 TEASPOON NUTMEG

1/4 CUP SHORTENING

1 CUP SUGAR

1 EGG

1 CUP BRAN OR BRAN FLAKES

1-1/2 CUPS WELL-MASHED RIPE BANANA (ABOUT 3 LARGE ONES)

1 TEASPOON VANILLA

2 TABLESPOONS WATER

1/2 CUP CHOPPED NUTS

HEAT OVEN TO 350 DEGREES. GREASE A 9 x 5 x 3 INCH LOAF PAN. SIFT FLOUR, BAKING POWDER, SODA, SALT AND NUTMEG. CREAM SHORTENING AND SUGAR TOGETHER. ADD EGG AND BEAT UNTIL FLUFFY. STIR IN BRAN, BANANA, VANILLA, WATER AND NUTS. ADD DRY INGREDIENTS, AND STIR JUST TO BLEND. SPOON INTO PREPARED PAN, AND SPREAD EVENLY. BAKE 50 - 60 MINUTES, OR UNTIL A TOOTHPICK STUCK IN CENTER COMES OUT CLEAN. REMOVE FROM PAN AND COOL ON CAKE RACK.

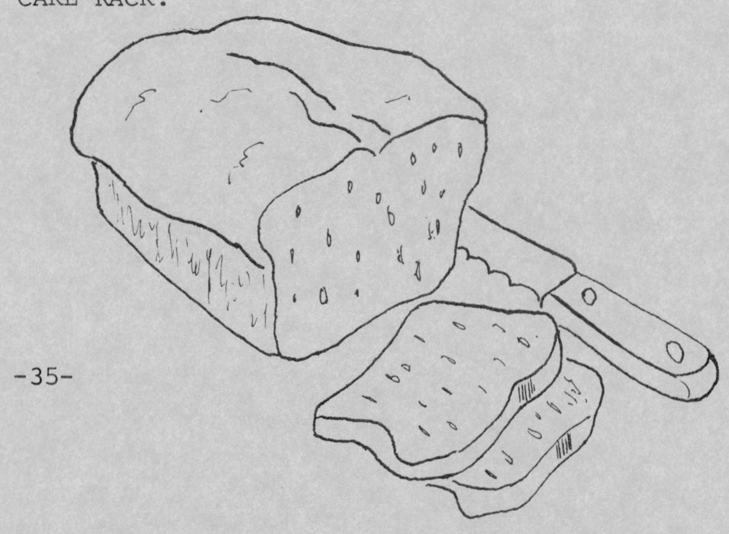

ADDITIONAL FAVOURITE RECIPES

ADDITIONAL FAVOURITE RECIPES

FAMILY LUNCHES

IT'S A LONG TIME AGO (I'M NOT TELLING HOW LONG) THAT A YOUNG, SPINDLY-LEGGED GIRL RAN DOWN THE TREE SHADED STREET AND BURST INTO THE DOOR WITH A "WHAT'S FOR LUNCH?" DESPITE THE TIME SPAN, MY TASTE BUDS STILL REMEMBER THE DELICIOUS, PIPING HOT SOUPS AND HOMEMADE BREAD THAT AWAITED US WHEN WE GOT HOME FROM SCHOOL. THOSE WERE THE HAPPY DAYS!

TODAY, WITH NUMEROUS WORKING MOTHERS, MANY FAMILIES AREN'T TOGETHER FOR THE NOON-HOUR MEAL. BUT FOR THOSE FAMILIES FORTUNATE ENOUGH TO HAVE A MOTHER WHO IS ABLE TO BE HOME TO MAKE NUTRITIOUS, APPETIZING LUNCHES WITH LEFT-OVERS, FRESH IN-SEASON VEGETABLES AND FRUIT OR THE WEEK'S "SPECIALS" - SALMON, TUNA OR ANY OF THE MANY ITEMS INTENDED TO FIT YOUR FOOD BUDGET, THE FOLLOWING SUGGESTIONS ARE OFFERED. SOME OF THEM AREN'T NEW OR DIFFERENT, BUT THEY MAY JUST FILL THE BILL NEXT MONDAY WHEN THE CLOCK CHIMES ELEVEN, YOU'VE JUST TAKEN THE FOURTH LOAD OF LAUNDRY OUT OF THE WASHER AND YOU FIND YOURSELF THINKING: "WHAT'LL I GIVE THE KIDS FOR LUNCH?"

MACARONI-FRANKS CASSEROLE

THIS RECIPE STRETCHES A 225 g. PACKAGE OF KRAFT DINNER TO FEED 6 TO 8 HUNGRY MOUTHS. A REAL BONANZA IN THESE DAYS OF HIGH FOOD COSTS!

1 PACKAGE KRAFT DINNER
1 CUP SPAGHETTI SAUCE
2 TABLESPOONS CHOPPED GREEN PEPPER
2 TABLESPOONS GREEN ONION (CHOPPED)
4 WEINERS

MAKE UP THE KRAFT DINNER ACCORDING TO THE DIRECTIONS ON THE PACKAGE AND PUT IT IN A GREASED, 2-QUART CASSEROLE. CUT THE WEINERS IN BITE-SIZE PIECES AND PLACE OVER THE KRAFT DINNER. MIX THE GREEN PEPPER AND ONION IN WITH THE SPAGHETTI SAUCE AND POUR OVER WEINERS. BAKE FOR 1 HOUR AT 350 DEGREES.

"WHITE COLLAR" HOT DOGS

THIS IS A GOOD WAY TO USE UP ANY LEFT-OVER MASHED POTATOES AS WELL AS DRESS UP THE LOWLY WEINER.

WEINERS
MASHED POTATOES (OR LEFT-OVERS HEATED UP)
SALT AND PEPPER TO TASTE
MINCED ONION
GRATED CHEESE

"WHITE COLLAR" HOT DOGS - continued

SEASON THE MASHED POTATOES AND ADD MINCED ONION. SLIT THE WEINERS AND FILL THE CAVITY WITH THE POTATOES AND TOP WITH GRATED CHEESE. BAKE IN 350 DEGREE OVEN UNTIL THEY ARE HEATED THROUGH AND THE CHEESE IS MELTED AND GOLDEN.

SAUERKRAUT IS ALSO A GOOD WEINER FILLER.

HOT TUNA SANDWICH

EVERYONE RAVES OVER THIS - AND YOU WILL TOO!

2 CANS FLAKED TUNA

4 HARD COOKED EGGS, MASHED

3 TABLESPOONS ONION, CHOPPED

1/4 CUP OLIVES (CHOPPED)

2/3 CUP MAYONNAISE

MIX ALL TOGETHER AND CHILL FOR 12 HOURS.

TOPPING: 5 OUNCES CHEDDAR CHEESE
1/4 POUND OF BUTTER

MIX CHEESE AND BUTTER AND SET ASIDE. PUT FILLING BETWEEN 2 SLICES OF BREAD (CRUST OFF). TOP WITH SPREAD AND BAKE IN 350 DEGREE OVEN FOR ABOUT 10 MINUTES, OR UNTIL TOPPING BUBBLES AND YOU ARE SURE FILLING IS HEATED THROUGH. DELICIOUS!

6 SERVINGS.

POTATO AND FISH CAKES

MY MOTHER USED TO MAKE THESE FOR US WHEN WE WERE GOING TO SCHOOL. IT REALLY STRETCHES A TIN OF SALMON, TUNA, ETC., AND USES UP LEFT-OVER MASHED POTATOES.

1/2 CUP CHOPPED ONION	1 EGG
2 TABLESPOONS BUTTER	1/2 TEASPOON SALT
2 CUPS MASHED POTATOES	Pepper
1 - 1# CAN SALMON, TUNA, ETC.	FINE BREAD CRUMBS

FAT FOR FRYING

SAUTÉ ONION IN BUTTER AND ADD TO THE REST OF THE INGREDIENTS, EXCEPT CRUMBS. SHAPE INTO CAKES. ROLL IN CRUMBS AND SAUTÉ IN HOT FAT UNTIL GOLDEN (ABOUT 10 MINUTES). MAKES 6 GENEROUS SERVINGS.

ANY LEFTOVER MEAT OR VEGETABLES CAN ALSO BE USED IN PLACE OF FISH.

PIZZA SANDWICH MIX

EVELYN, OUR SUPER OFFICE COOKER, GAVE ME THIS RECIPE. IT CAN BE USED AT VARIOUS LUNCH FUNCTIONS - BRIDGE AND NEIGHBOURHOOD (ON SMALL ROLLS) OR FAMILY (ON HAMBURG ROLLS). TREAT YOUR FAMILY ONE DAY SOON - THEY'RE DELICIOUS!

PUT THE FOLLOWING INGREDIENTS THROUGH FOOD CHOPPER:

- 1/2 POUND SMOKED BACK BACON
- 1/2 POUND CHEDDAR CHEESE
- 1 MEDIUM ONION
- 1 GREEN PEPPER

ADD THE FOLLOWING, AND MIX WELL:

- 1 EGG
- 1 TEASPOON WORCESTERSHIRE SAUCE

SPREAD ON ROLL HALVES AND COOK UNDER BROILER UNTIL JUST BEFORE THEY ARE GOING TO BURN! 6 SERVINGS.

BEEF ON A BUN

THIS RECIPE SOLVED MY LEFT-OVER ROAST BEEF PROBLEM. UNLESS I HAVE A BIG CROWD FOR SUNDAY DINNER OR A VERY TINY ROAST, IT APPEARS ON THE TABLE ON MONDAY NIGHT WITH THE LEFT-OVER POTATOES, GRAVY AND

VEGETABLES. THAT I LIKE. TUESDAY NIGHT, AND SOMETIMES WEDNESDAY, IT'S ON CENTER STAGE AGAIN, THIS TIME DISGUISED BY TWO PIECES OF BREAD AND LOTS OF GRAVY. THURSDAY IT GETS SERVED COLD, EITHER ALONGSIDE A SALAD OR IN BETWEEN TWO SLICES OF BREAD. BY THIS TIME I'M TIRED OF IT AND HAVE USED UP MY WEEK'S SUPPLY OF CALORIES. "BEEF ON A BUN" MAKES ITS DEBUT EARLIER IN THE WEEK AND IS A TREAT, EITHER SERVED ON A BUN, OVER RICE BUTTERED NOODLES OR MASHED POTATOES. IT IS ALSO DELICIOUS MADE WITH LEFT-OVER ROAST PORK. MAKE IT UP THE DAY BEFORE AND REFRIGERATE OVERNIGHT.

MIX TOGETHER:

2 TABLESPOONS SUGAR
2 TABLESPOONS VINEGAR
2 TEASPOONS PREPARED MUSTARD
2 TEASPOONS LEMON JUICE
1 TEASPOON SALT
1 TEASPOON PAPRIKA
1/4 TEASPOON PEPPER
3/4 CUP WATER
4 TABLESPOONS BUTTER
1 MED. ONION, SLICED THIN
1/4 GREEN PEPPER, CUT IN STRIPS

SIMMER, UNCOVERED FOR 20 MINUTES, AND ADD:

1/2 CUP KETCHUP
1 TEASPOON MONOSODIUM GLUTOMATE
1-1/2 TO 2 CUPS COOKED ROAST BEEF CUT IN STRIPS

REFRIGERATE. ABOUT 30 MINUTES BEFORE SERVING, SIMMER SLOWLY TO HEAT. TO SERVE, SPRINKLE WITH CHOPPED PARSLEY AND CELERY LEAVES.

FRENCH ONION SOUP

A FRENCH LADY ONCE GAVE ME THE RECIPE FOR HER FABULOUS ONION SOUP, BUT I GOT HALF-WAY THROUGH THE MAZE OF INGREDIENTS AND THOUGHT "THIS IS TOO MUCH WORK FOR ME!" SINCE THEN, I'VE JUST USED THIS EASIER VARIETY. SMALL WONDER SOME FRENCH CHEFS LOOK AS IF THEY HAVE SLAVED ALL DAY OVER A HOT STOVE. THEY PROBABLY HAVE!

1 CAN (10 OUNCES) CONDENSED ONION SOUP
1 SOUP CAN WATER
2 OR 3 SLICES FRENCH STICK (ABOUT 1/2" THICK)
BUTTER
GRATED PARMESAN CHEESE

COMBINE SOUP AND WATER. HEAT. LET SIMMER A FEW MINUTES. ARRANGE BREAD ON COOKIE SHEET; SPREAD WITH BUTTER AND SPRINKLE WITH PARMESAN CHEESE. BROIL 'TIL LIGHTLY BROWNED. POUR SOUP INTO BOWLS; TOP EACH WITH A SLICE OF FRENCH STICK - 2 TO 3 SERVINGS.

POTATO SOUP

IS THERE ANYTHING MORE SATISFYING ON A COLD WINTER'S DAY THAN A STEAMING HOT BOWL OF HOMEMADE SOUP? I GET A LITTLE STEAMY-EYED THINKING OF THE FUN WE USED TO HAVE IN THE WINTER - RUSHING OUT OF SCHOOL AT NOON AND TEARING DOWN CARLTON STREET WITH THE BOYS IN PURSUIT, PELTING US WITH SNOWBALLS; BEGGING CHUNKS OF ICE TO SUCK FROM MR. DOYLE'S ICE TRUCK; STARTING A SNOWMAN AT THE ANGLICAN CHURCH AND HAVING A JOLLY, FAT SANTA CLAUS BY THE TIME WE GOT TO OUR CORNER. WHEN WE ARRIVED HOME, THERE WAS NEARLY ALWAYS A BIG POT OF SOUP ON THE STOVE, AND HOW WE LOVED IT!

6 SLICES BACON
1/2 CUP CHOPPED ONION
1/2 CUP FINELY CHOPPED CARROTS
1 CUP THINLY SLICED CELERY
3 CUPS CUBED POTATOES
2 TABLESPOONS PARSLEY
1-1/2 CUPS CHICKEN BROTH (MAY USE BOUILLON CUBES)
3/4 TEASPOON SALT
1/8 TEASPOON PEPPER
3-1/2 CUPS MILK
1/4 CUP FLOUR
1/2 CUP MILK
CHOPPED PARSLEY

COOK BACON IN LARGE KETTLE UNTIL ALMOST CRISP. REMOVE FROM KETTLE AND RESERVE. IN REMAINING BACON FAT, SAUTÉ ONION UNTIL TENDER. ADD NEXT 7 INGREDIENTS. COVER AND SIMMER UNTIL VEGETABLES ARE TENDER -

POTATO SOUP - continued

ABOUT 15 MINUTES. ADD 3-1/2 CUPS MILK AND HEAT. DO NOT ALLOW TO BOIL. BLEND FLOUR AND 1/2 CUP MILK AND ADD IT, STIRRING CONSTANTLY, INTO SOUP. COOK UNTIL BUBBLY AND SLIGHTLY THICKENED. STIR IN RESERVED BACON AND CHOPPED PARSLEY.

BROILED FRUIT AND HAM-WICHES

EVEN FAMILY LUNCHES NEED A BIT OF SPICE TO MAKE THEM INTERESTING. THIS SANDWICH WILL DO JUST THAT TO AN ORDINARY WEEK-DAY TWELVE O'CLOCK REPAST.

4 ENGLISH MUFFINS, SPLIT
1/4 CUP MARGARINE, SOFTENED
2 TEASPOONS PREPARED MUSTARD
8 SLICES LUNCHEON MEAT OR COOKED HAM
1 - 10-OUNCE CAN CRUSHED PINEAPPLE, DRAINED
OR FRESH APPLE SLICES
8 SLICES SWISS CHEESE

ARRANGE MUFFIN HALVES ON BAKING SHEET. COMBINE MARGARINE AND MUSTARD, SPREAD ON EACH MUFFIN HALF. TOP WITH A FOLDED SLICE OF MEAT, CRUSHED PINEAPPLE OR APPLE SLICES AND FOLDED CHEESE SLICE. BROIL 'TIL CHEESE BEGINS TO BUBBLE.

BAKED EGGS AU GRATIN

BET THE FAMILY WILL LOVE THIS ONE.

1/4 CUP DRY BREAD CRUMBS	1 TABLESPOON MILK
1 TABLESPOON BUTTER OR MARGARINE, MELTED	1 TABLESPOON INSTANT MINCED ONION
4 HARD-COOKED EGGS, SLICED	1/2 TEASPOON SALT
3 SLICES BACON, DICED	1/4 TEASPOON PAPRIKA
1 CUP DAIRY SOUR CREAM	1/8 TEASPOON PEPPER

1/2 CUP SHREDDED CHEDDAR CHEESE

HEAT OVEN TO 350 DEGREES. TOSS BREAD CRUMBS IN BUTTER AND DIVIDE AMONG 4 BUTTERED 10-OUNCE BAKING DISHES. LAYER EGG SLICES OVER CRUMBS. FRY BACON UNTIL CRISP; DRAIN. STIR TOGETHER BACON, SOUR CREAM, MILK, ONION AND SEASONINGS; SPOON OVER EGGS. TOP WITH CHEESE. BAKE UNCOVERED 10 TO 15 MINUTES OR UNTIL CHEESE IS MELTED. SERVES 4.

EASY LASAGNA

I'VE YET TO RUN ACROSS ANYONE WHO DOESN'T LIKE LASAGNA, ALTHOUGH MY FIRST EXPERIENCE WITH IT WASN'T A ROARING SUCCESS. I HAD INVITED MY COTTAGE NEIGHBOURS OVER FOR A "BEFORE-THE-SHOW" SUPPER AND THOUGHT THAT LASAGNA WOULD

EASY LASAGNA - continued

BE EASY TO MAKE AND PLEASE TEENAGERS' APPETITES. WELL, THEY LIKED ITALIAN FOOD, BUT IT TOOK ME ALL AFTERNOON TO PREPARE IT AND IT WAS ALMOST A DISASTER. NOVICE THAT I WAS, I FOLLOWED THE COOK-BOOK STEP BY STEP. "LAYER THE NOODLES, COTTAGE CHEESE, MEAT AND SAUCE MIXTURE, ETC. ETC.," THE RECIPE SAID. SO I LAYERED THE NOODLES AND THE MULTITUDE OF OTHER INGREDIENTS. IT LOOKED BEAUTIFUL - AND PROFESSIONAL. I BUSIED MYSELF SETTING THE TABLE WITH A RED-AND-WHITE CHECKERED CLOTH, PUT CANDLES IN WINE BASKETS, CHILLED A BOTTLE OF CHIANTI AND HUMMED A FEW BARS OF LE TRAVIATA. THE TIMER SOUNDED; MY MASTERPIECE WAS FINISHED. OR SO I THOUGHT. THE TESTING FORK STRUCK SOMETHING HARD, AND UNCOOKED .... THE NOODLES! THE RECIPE HADN'T SAID "COOK THE NOODLES FIRST" SO I DIDN'T. LUCKILY, THE GUESTS WEREN'T DUE TO ARRIVE FOR ANOTHER HOUR-AND-a-HALF, SO THERE WAS TIME TO CONCOCT SOME TOMATO SAUCE AND THROW IT IN THE CASSEROLE. THE NOODLES EVENTUALLY SOFTENED AND THE CONTINENTAL SUPPER SURVIVED, BUT I TOOK A LOT OF TEASING, AND THE BOYS ASKED FOR STEAK KNIVES!

EASY LASAGNA - continued

EVEN THOUGH I NOW KNOW HOW TO MAKE LASAGNA, THE PREPARATION IS TIME CONSUMING, SO WE GIVE YOU THIS EASIER VERSION. ACCORDING TO THE RECIPE, IT SERVES 4 PEOPLE - BUT IT REALLY FEEDS 4 VERY HUNGRY PEOPLE.

2 CUPS REGULAR NOODLES

1 CUP COTTAGE CHEESE

1/2 POUND GROUND BEEF

4 SLICES MOZZARELLA CHEESE, CUT IN STRIPS

1 CAN (ABOUT 11 OZ.) SPAGHETTI SAUCE WITH MUSHROOMS

1/4 CUP GRATED PARMESAN CHEESE

COOK NOODLES UNTIL TENDER. DRAIN, AND SPOON INTO A GREASED, SHALLOW 6-CUP BAKING DISH. SPREAD COTTAGE CHEESE OVER NOODLES; BREAK UP GROUND BEEF AND SPRINKLE ON TOP. PLACE HALF EACH OF THE CHEESE STRIPS AND SPAGHETTI SAUCE ON TOP; REPEAT WITH REMAINING CHEESE STRIPS AND SAUCE. SPRINKLE WITH PARMESAN CHEESE. BAKE IN 375-DEGREE OVEN FOR 45 MINUTES, OR UNTIL BUBBLY IN CENTER AND THE TOP IS GOLDEN-BROWN.

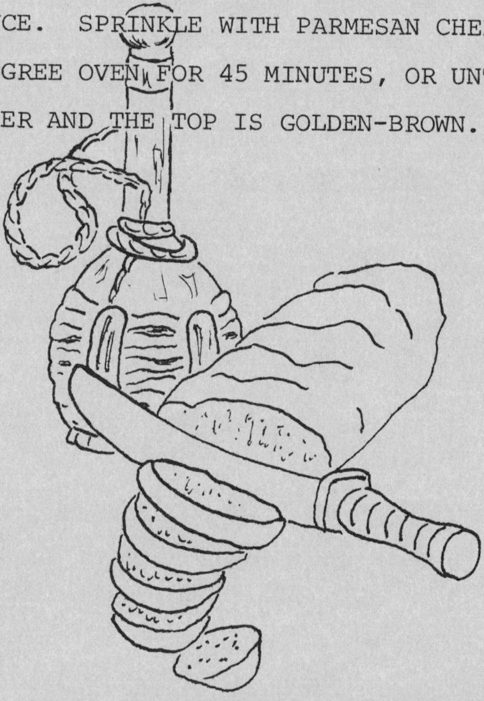

POTATO-ZUCCHINI PANCAKES

2 GOOD-SIZED POTATOES, PEELED

1 UNPEELED MEDIUM ZUCCHINI, SHREDDED

1 EGG, BEATEN LIGHTLY

2 TABLESPOONS FLOUR

1/2 TEASPOON SALT

1/2 TEASPOON NUTMEG

PEPPER TO TASTE (FRESHLY GROUND, IF POSSIBLE)

2 - 3 TABLESPOONS BUTTER

2 - 3 TABLESPOONS OIL

SHRED POTATOES AND PUT IN BOWL OF COLD WATER. WHEN READY TO COOK, DRAIN WELL, PLACE POTATOES ON A TOWEL AND SQUEEZE GENTLY TO REMOVE MOISTURE. PUT POTATOES IN MIXING BOWL, ADD ZUCCHINI, EGG, FLOUR, SALT, NUTMEG AND PEPPER AND MIX. HEAT 1 TABLESPOON EACH OF BUTTER AND OIL IN LARGE SKILLET UNTIL VERY HOT. WHEN SKILLET IS READY, SPOON MIXTURE INTO IT (3 TABLE-SPOONS FOR EACH PANCAKE), COOK UNTIL GOLDEN AND CRISP ON EACH SIDE. ADD THE REST OF THE OIL AND BUTTER TO THE PAN AND COOK REST OF PANCAKES. THESE CAN BE MADE AHEAD OF TIME AND REHEATED IN A 350-DEGREE OVEN FOR ABOUT 10 MINUTES.

TOASTED DEVILLED HAMBURGERS

1 POUND LEAN GROUND CHUCK

1/3 CUP CHILI SAUCE

1-1/2 TEASPOONS PREPARED MUSTARD

1-1/2 TEASPOONS HORSERADISH

1 TEASPOON MINCED ONION

1-1/2 TEASPOONS WORCESTERSHIRE SAUCE

1 TEASPOON SALT

SPECK OF PEPPER

8 SLICES OF WHITE BREAD

MIX ALL INGREDIENTS, EXCEPT BREAD. TRIM CRUSTS FROM BREAD AND TOAST ONE SIDE UNDER THE BROILER. SPREAD UNTOASTED SIDE OF EACH WITH SOME OF MEAT MIXTURE, SPREADING RIGHT TO EDGES. BROIL FOR 6 MINUTES. CUT EACH INTO 3 STRIPS. MIGHTY GOOD!

BUBBLING FISH BAKE

MY FRIEND, NORMA, WHOSE RECIPES APPEARED IN "WITH A PINCH OF PINE CONES AND CHIPMUNKS," SUPPLIED THIS FISH DISH. I KNEW IT WOULD BE DELICIOUS; NORMA HAS HAD A LOT OF EXPERIENCE COOKING FOR HER FAMILY AND THEIR NUMEROUS FRIENDS WHO ARE ALWAYS "DROPPING BY" AT MEAL TIME - ME INCLUDED!

BUBBLING FISH BAKE - continued

1 CUP CHOPPED ONION

2 TABLESPOONS BUTTER

1 CUP (10-OZ. CAN) CONDENSED CREAM OF CELERY OR MUSHROOM SOUP

1/2 CUP MILK

1 CUP CHEDDAR CHEESE, GRATED

2 CUPS COOKED MACARONI OR NOODLES

1 CUP (7-3/4 OZ. CAN) SALMON OR TUNA, DRAINED AND FLAKED

2 TABLESPOONS BUTTERED BREAD CRUMBS

COOK ONION IN BUTTER UNTIL TENDER. STIR IN SOUP, MILK, 3/4 CUP CHEESE, MACARONI AND FISH. POUR INTO 1-1/2 QT. CASSEROLE AND TOP WITH BREAD CRUMBS AND REMAINING CHEESE. BAKE IN A 350-DEGREE OVEN FOR 30 MINUTES OR UNTIL LIGHTLY BROWN AND BUBBLING.

SAUCY WEINERS

12 WEINERS

1 CUP UNSWEETENED JUICE - APPLE OR PINEAPPLE

1/8 TEASPOON CHILI POWDER

5 SLICES BACON, COOKED BUT NOT CRISP

1/2 CUP KETCHUP

1/2 CUP CHOPPED ONION

3/4 CUP GREEN PEPPER, CHOPPED

COOK BACON UNTIL DONE BUT NOT CRISP. ADD ONIONS AND COOK UNTIL TENDER. STIR IN KETCHUP, CHILI POWDER AND JUICE. SCORE WEINERS DIAGONALLY EVERY INCH AND ADD TO OTHER INGREDIENTS. COVER AND BRING TO A BOIL, ADD GREEN PEPPER AND SIMMER 10 MINUTES. SERVE OVER HOT RICE OR SPAGHETTI. SERVES 6.

WEINER KABOBS

WEINERS, CUT IN THIRDS
PINEAPPLE CHUNKS
WHOLE SWEET PICKLES
BARBECUE SAUCE
HOT DOG ROLLS, SPLIT AND GRILLED
CHEESE WHIZ

FOR EACH KABOB, ARRANGE WEINERS, PINEAPPLE AND PICKLES ON A SKEWER. BRUSH WITH BARBECUE SAUCE AND PLACE UNDER BROILER, BASTING OCCASIONALLY WITH SAUCE DURING COOKING PERIOD. SERVE IN ROLLS WHICH HAVE BEEN TOASTED UNDER THE BROILER AND SPREAD WITH CHEESE WHIZ. YOUR "HOT DOG CROWD" WILL LOVE THESE!

NEOPOLITAN SUB

1 POUND GROUND BEEF
1 TABLESPOON MARGARINE
1/2 CUP CHOPPED ONION
1 - 7-1/2 OUNCE CAN TOMATO SAUCE
1/2 TEASPOON OREGANO
1/2 TEASPOON SALT
1/4 TEASPOON GARLIC SALT
HOT DOG BUNS
MOZZARELLA CHEESE SLICES, CUT IN STRIPS

BROWN BEEF IN MARGARINE - ADD ONION AND COOK UNTIL TENDER. ADD TOMATO SAUCE AND SEASONINGS; SIMMER 15 MINUTES. SPOON MEAT SAUCE ON HOT DOG ROLL HALVES

NEOPOLITAN SUB - continued

AND TOP WITH CHEESE STRIPS. BROIL UNTIL CHEESE BEGINS TO MELT. WHEN THE TOMATOES ARE RIPE ON THE VINES, GARNISH WITH CHERRY TOMATOES OR A TOMATO SLICE. Mmmmmmmm Mmmmmmmm GOOD!

CHICKEN CASSEROLE

A GOOD WAY TO USE UP CHICKEN OR TURKEY LEFT-OVERS.

- 1/4 CUP ONIONS
- 2 CUPS CHOPPED CELERY
- 2 CUPS DICED CHICKEN
- 1 CAN CREAM OF MUSHROOM SOUP
- 3 HARD COOKED EGGS
- 1/2 CUP SALAD DRESSING
- 1/2 CUP SLIVERED, TOASTED ALMONDS
- 1/2 CUP FROZEN PEAS
- POTATO CHIPS, CRUSHED
- GRATED CHEESE

SAUTÉ THE ONION AND CELERY IN A LITTLE BUTTER. COMBINE WITH THE REMAINDER OF THE INGREDIENTS (EXCEPT CHIPS AND CHEESE) AND PLACE IN BUTTERED CASSEROLE. COVER WITH CRUSHED POTATO CHIPS AND GRATED CHEESE. THIS CAN BE ASSEMBLED THE NIGHT BEFORE, ADDING THE TOPPING BEFORE IT GOES IN THE OVEN. HEAT IN MODERATE OVEN.

HAMBURGER HOT POT

WHILE THE PRICE OF HAMBURG HAS RISEN ALONG WITH OTHER FOOD PRODUCTS, COMBINED WITH VEGETABLES, IT STILL IS A GOOD "STRETCHER."

- 4 MEDIUM-SIZE POTATOES, PARED AND SLICED THIN
- 3 CARROTS, SLICED THIN
- 1-1/2 POUNDS GROUND BEEF
- 3 MEDIUM-SIZE ONIONS, PEELED AND SLICED THIN
- 1 TEASPOON SALT
- 1/4 TEASPOON PEPPER
- 2 TABLESPOONS BUTTER OR MARGARINE
- 2 TABLESPOONS CHOPPED PARSLEY
- 1/2 CUP CANNED CONDENSED BEEF BROTH

PLACE ONE-THIRD OF THE POTATO SLICES IN THE BOTTOM OF A BUTTERED ELECTRIC FRY PAN (OR IN REGULAR COVERED SKILLET OVER LOW HEAT); TOP WITH EVEN LAYERS OF HALF OF THE GROUND BEEF, HALF OF THE CARROTS AND HALF OF THE ONION SLICES. REPEAT LAYERS, ENDING WITH POTATO SLICES. SPRINKLE WITH SALT AND PEPPER; DOT WITH BUTTER OR MARGARINE; SPRINKLE WITH PARSLEY. POUR BEEF BROTH OVER. COVER. SET HEAT AT 225 DEGREES AND SIMMER FOR 1 HOUR, OR UNTIL POTATOES AND CARROTS ARE TENDER. SERVES 6.

WE SUDDENLY REALIZED WE'D FORGOTTEN TO INCLUDE DESSERTS IN THIS SECTION, SO WE RIFLED OUR RECIPE BOXES AND CAME UP WITH SOME "FAMILY" DESSERTS.

CARAMEL PUDDING

MY MOTHER USED TO MAKE A CARAMEL PUDDING THAT WE THOUGHT WAS VERY SPECIAL. SHE DIDN'T HAVE A RECIPE FOR IT, BUT I CAN STILL SEE HER MIXING LOTS OF BUTTER WITH BROWN SUGAR IN A BIG, BLACK FRYING PAN AND ADDING MILK. I OFTEN WISH THAT I HAD WRITTEN THE INGREDIENTS AND THE METHOD DOWN (ALONG WITH NUMEROUS OTHER RECIPES OF HERS). MARILYN CAME UP WITH HER RECIPE, WHICH SOUNDS SIMILAR. I'M GOING TO MAKE IT TOMORROW.

2 TABLESPOONS BUTTER	1 TABLESPOON FLOUR
1 CUP BROWN SUGAR	2-1/2 TABLESPOONS CORN STARCH
1/2 TEASPOON SALT	2 EGGS
3 CUPS MILK	VANILLA

PUT FIRST THREE ITEMS IN SKILLET AND COOK, STIRRING CONSTANTLY, OVER LOW HEAT UNTIL THE MIXTURE IS CARAMELIZED TO A RICH, GOLDEN BROWN SYRUP. <u>VERY SLOWLY</u> ADD 2 CUPS MILK AND HEAT TO BOILING, AGAIN

CARAMEL PUDDING - continued

STIRRING CONSTANTLY. REMOVE FROM HEAT. MIX TOGETHER REMAINING 1 CUP MILK WITH THE FLOUR AND CORN STARCH AND MIX SMOOTH. RETURN SKILLET TO HEAT AND SLOWLY ADD COLD MILK MIXTURE TO SKILLET, STIRRING CONSTANTLY UNTIL SMOOTH AND THICKENED. (SOUNDS LIKE AN AWFUL LOT OF STIRRING!) BEAT EGGS AND ADD ONE CUP HOT MIXTURE SLOWLY TO EGGS. RETURN THIS MIXTURE TO SKILLET AND COOK, BUT DO NOT BOIL, FOR 2 MINUTES. REMOVE FROM HEAT AND ADD VANILLA TO TASTE. SERVES 8.

FRUIT COCKTAIL DELIGHT

1 - 14-OUNCE CAN FRUIT COCKTAIL
1 CUP FLOUR
1 CUP SUGAR
1/2 TEASPOON SALT
1 TEASPOON BAKING SODA
1 EGG
1 TEASPOON ALMOND FLAVORING
6 TABLESPOONS BROWN SUGAR
6 TABLESPOONS CHOPPED NUTS

DRAIN THE FRUIT COCKTAIL AND SET ASIDE 1/4 CUP OF THE JUICE. SIFT TOGETHER THE FLOUR, SUGAR, SALT AND SODA; ADD THE EGG (UNBEATEN) AND THE FRUIT JUICE; THEN ADD THE FRUIT COCKTAIL AND THE ALMOND FLAVORING. SPREAD IN 9 x 9 WELL-GREASED PAN. OVER THIS SPREAD THE BROWN SUGAR AND THE CHOPPED NUTS. BAKE AT 350 FOR ABOUT 45 MINS. MAY BE SERVED WARM OR COLD WITH ICE CREAM.

JELLO SNOW

I WELL REMEMBER HOW PROUD I WAS WHEN I LEARNED TO MAKE LEMON SNOW AT HOME ECONOMICS. THIS IS A DIFFERENT VARIETY OF "SNOW" BUT IT'S JUST AS TASTY.

1 - 3-OUNCE LEMON JELLY POWDER (OR ANY DESIRED FLAVOUR)

2 - EGG WHITES

MAKE JELLY ACCORDING TO PACKAGE DIRECTIONS. WHEN IT BEGINS TO SET, FOLD IN EGG WHITES WHICH HAVE BEEN STIFFLY BEATEN. FINISH SETTING EITHER IN INDIVIDUAL DESSERT DISHES OR ONE LARGE BOWL. SERVE WITH CUSTARD SAUCE.

CUSTARD SAUCE:

1 CUP MILK

2 EGG YOLKS

2 TABLESPOONS SUGAR

DASH SALT

1/2 TEASPOON VANILLA

HEAT MILK OVER DOUBLE BOILER. BEAT EGG YOLKS WITH A FORK AND STIR IN SUGAR AND SALT. SLOWLY ADD HOT MILK TO YOLK MIXTURE, STIRRING CONSTANTLY. RETURN TO DOUBLE BOILER AND COOK OVER HOT WATER, STIRRING CONTINUALLY, UNTIL MIXTURE COATS A METAL SPOON WITH A THIN FILM OF CUSTARD. DO NOT OVER-COOK AS IT WILL CURDLE. COOL AND STIR IN VANILLA. CHILL WELL.

Very Good

APPLE-COCONUT CRISP

6 - 8 PARED APPLES
1-1/4 CUPS SUGAR
1 EGG
1/2 CUP BISCUIT MIX
1 TABLESPOON MELTED BUTTER
1/2 TEASPOON VANILLA
1/2 CUP COCONUT
PINCH OF SALT

SLICE APPLES INTO SHALLOW, GREASED BAKING DISH. SPRINKLE WITH 1/2 CUP SUGAR. BAKE AT 325 DEGREES FOR 10 - 15 MINUTES. BEAT EGG, 3/4 CUP SUGAR, BISCUIT MIX, BUTTER, VANILLA, COCONUT AND SALT TOGETHER. SPREAD OVER APPLES AND BAKE 30 MINUTES OR UNTIL APPLES ARE TENDER. SERVE WITH ICE CREAM OR TOP WITH WHIPPED CREAM.

ADDITIONAL FAVOURITE RECIPES

ADDITIONAL FAVOURITE RECIPES

ADDITIONAL FAVOURITE RECIPES

GUEST LUNCHEONS

IT'S SATURDAY MORNING. I FIND MYSELF UNABLE TO LUXURIATE IN BED VERY LONG AFTER THE FOOTSTEPS OF THE MORNING PAPER CARRIER SOUND ON THE FRONT STEPS. SO I ENJOY A LEISURELY BREAKFAST, THEN THROW THE FIRST OF THREE LOADS INTO THE WASHER, DECIDE MY WEDNESDAY HAIR-DO LOOKS WILTED SO I TRY OUT THAT EXPENSIVE, NEW SHAMPOO THAT'S SUPPOSED TO SHAVE YEARS OFF MY AGE, AND PUT MY CROWNING GLORY UP IN CURLERS. ALL THIS WHILE I'M STILL CLOTHED IN MY LONG-TIME FAVOURITE ROBE WITH THE RIP DOWN THE SIDE. THE KITCHEN CURTAINS LOOK AS IF THEY COULD STAND A BIT OF FRESHENING UP. SO DO THE DINING ROOM ONES. INTO THE WASHER THEY ALL GO. THEN THE 'PHONE RINGS; AN OLD SCHOOL FRIEND FROM OUT WEST IS VISITING FRIENDS IN TOWN AND SHE WONDERS IF I'M GOING TO BE HOME AROUND NOON. IS THAT REALLY MY VOICE I HEAR SAYING "BUT I INSIST THAT YOU COME FOR LUNCH. I WON'T FUSS - I PROMISE."

OH BOY! HELEN WAS ALWAYS A HOUSE SLAVE. SHE WOULDN'T BE CAUGHT DEAD WITH HER HAIR IN CURLERS AT HIGH NOON, BUT THE CURTAINS HAD TO BE DRIED, IRONED AND HUNG, THE CARPETS VACUUMED, AND WHY DIDN'T I CLEAN THE SILVER LAST WEEK WHEN THE BRIDGE CLUB CAME? THERE SIMPLY WASN'T ENOUGH TIME. THE CURLERS WOULD HAVE TO STAY IN PLACE - BETTER THAT THAN STRINGY, WET HAIR IN THE MIDDLE OF MARCH.

(IF IT WERE JULY, I COULD ALWAYS USE A DIP IN THE NEIGHBOUR'S POOL AS AN EXCUSE.)

AT LEAST I CAN WHIP UP A QUICK, TASTY LUNCH WHICH, HOPEFULLY, WILL OVERSHADOW MY SHORTCOMINGS.

WITH AMPLE NOTICE, IT'S FUN TO DRESS UP YOUR DINING ROOM TABLE TO LOOK LIKE AN ILLUSTRATION FROM HOUSE BEAUTIFUL AND SEARCH YOUR RECIPE FILE FOR EASY, DELICIOUS, SOMETIMES A TRIFLE EXTRAVAGANT LUNCHEON DISHES.

BUFFETS ARE INTERESTING TOO - EITHER AN 11 O'CLOCK BRUNCH AFTER EARLY CHURCH OR A NEIGHBOURHOOD GET-TOGETHER.

ANOTHER FORM OF LUNCH IS A SIMPLE ONE ON THE CARD TABLE BETWEEN RUBBERS, BUT PERHAPS NOT AS EASY ON THE DIGESTIVE SYSTEM!

ANYWAY, MARILYN AND I DECIDED IT WAS HIGH TIME WE GOT ALL OUR FAVOURITE LUNCHEON RECIPES TOGETHER IN ONE BOOK, SO HERE THEY ARE.

ENJOY YOURSELF!

THE STYLEISHNESS WITH WHICH YOU ENTERTAIN AT NOON IS NOT ONLY DETERMINED BY THE FOOD YOU SERVE, BUT BY THE TABLE SETTING. YOUR BEST CHINA, CRYSTAL GOBLETS AND A FRESH FLORAL CENTERPIECE MAKE EVEN THE PLAINEST MEAL SOMEWHAT SPECIAL. BUT, ALAS, ALL THE FINE CHINA AND SILVER YOU HAVE CAN'T DISGUISE A DULL, TASTELESS MEAL. LISTEN TO THE VOICE OF EXPERIENCE! I GUESS IT'S BEST TO CONCENTRATE ON YOUR COOKING, AND IF YOU HAVE TIME TO SPARE, PICK SOME FRESH FLOWERS FROM THE GARDEN OR WILD FLOWERS FROM A FIELD AND POLISH UP THOSE WEDDING GIFTS!

SPARKLING ROSÉ

ASSORTED FRUIT SALAD WITH
HONEY-CREAM DRESSING

CHEESE PUFFS

ENGLISH TOFFEE DESSERT

COFFEE

ASSORTED FRUIT SALAD WITH HONEY-CREAM DRESSING

MIX TOGETHER IN LARGE BOWL, CHUNKS OF WATERMELON, CANTELOUPE, PINEAPPLE, SLICED BANANAS, STRAWBERRIES, KIWI FRUIT, ETC. POUR HONEY-CREAM DRESSING OVER IT. SERVE IN LETTUCE CUPS ON INDIVIDUAL SALAD PLATES.

HONEY-CREAM DRESSING:

COMBINE AND CHILL -
- 1/2 CUP DAIRY SOUR CREAM
- 1 TABLESPOON HONEY
- 1 TABLESPOON ORANGE JUICE
- 1/2 TEASPOON ORANGE RIND (OPTIONAL)

IF YOU HAVE A LITTLE MORE TIME, THE FOLLOWING IS ALSO AN EXCELLENT DRESSING:

FRUIT SALAD DRESSING:

- 2 SLIGHTLY BEATEN EGGS
- 1/4 CUP GRANULATED SUGAR
- 1 TABLESPOON GRATED LEMON RIND
- 1/4 CUP LEMON JUICE
- 1 TABLESPOON GRATED ORANGE RIND
- 1/2 CUP ORANGE JUICE
- 1/2 CUP WHIPPING CREAM

COMBINE FIRST 6 INGREDIENTS IN TOP OF DOUBLE BOILER; COOK OVER SIMMERING WATER, STIRRING CONSTANTLY, 'TIL SMOOTHLY THICKENED. CHILL. BEAT WHIPPING CREAM 'TIL STIFF; FOLD IN CHILLED FRUIT CUSTARD. CHILL.

CHEESE PUFFS

THESE ARE DELICIOUS, AND THE BEST PART OF THEM IS THAT THEY ARE TO BE MADE THE DAY BEFORE YOU WANT TO SERVE THEM. A REAL BONUS FOR A BUSY HOSTESS!

1 LOAF UNSLICED SANDWICH BREAD - CRUSTS REMOVED AND CUT IN 1" CUBES
1 - 4-OUNCE PACKAGE CREAM CHEESE
1/4 POUND (1 CUP) GRATED, NIPPY CHEDDAR CHEESE
1/2 CUP BUTTER
2 STIFFLY BEATEN EGG WHITES

MELT CHEESES AND BUTTER IN DOUBLE BOILER. BEAT BY HAND UNTIL BLENDED. FOLD IN BEATEN EGG WHITES. DIP BREAD IN CHEESE MIXTURE AND PLACE ON WELL-GREASED COOKIE SHEET AND CHILL OVERNIGHT. BAKE AT 400 DEG. FOR 8 TO 10 MINUTES UNTIL PUFFY.

IF CHEESE MIXTURE SEEMS A LITTLE TOO THICK FOR DIPPING, ADD A LITTLE MORE BUTTER.

ENGLISH TOFFEE DESSERT

16 VANILLA WAFERS (1 CUP ROLLED)

3 EGGS, SEPARATED

1 CUP CHOPPED NUTS

1 CUP ICING SUGAR

1/4 POUND BUTTER

1-1/2 SQUARES BITTER CHOCOLATE

1/2 TEASPOON VANILLA

ROLL VANILLA WAFERS INTO CRUMBS AND MIX TOGETHER WITH CHOPPED NUTS. USING HALF OF THE MIXTURE, COVER THE BOTTOM OF A BUTTERED 9 x 9 PAN. CREAM BUTTER AND SUGAR, ADD BEATEN EGG YOLKS, MELTED CHOCOLATE AND VANILLA. FOLD IN BEATEN WHITES. POUR OVER WAFERS AND SPREAD REMAINING CRUMBS ON TOP. PUT IN REFRIGERATOR OVERNIGHT. CUT IN SQUARES AND SERVE WITH WHIPPED CREAM.

SERVES 9.

THE FOLLOWING MENU STARTED OUT TO BE A DIETER'S DELIGHT, BUT THEN I UPSET THE APPLE CART WITH MY PECAN-PINEAPPLE ICE BOX DESSERT.

VIRGINIA HAM SALAD

TOMATO WEDGES

ASSORTED "THIN" BREADS

PECAN-PINEAPPLE ICE BOX DESSERT

VIRGINIA HAM SALAD

NICE FOR A SPRING OR SUMMER LUNCHEON - WITH TOMATOES FRESH FROM THE GARDEN!

2/3 CUP UNCOOKED REGULAR RICE

1 TEASPOON SALT

BOILING WATER

1/2 CUP MAYONNAISE

1 TEASPOON GRATED ONION

1/2 TEASPOON SALT

PEPPER

1 CUP THIN STRIPS COOKED HAM

1 CUP THIN STRIPS SWISS CHEESE

2 TABLESPOONS FINELY CHOPPED DILL PICKLE

1 CUP COOKED FROZEN PEAS

LETTUCE

TOMATOES CUT IN WEDGES

VIRGINIA HAM SALAD - continued

COOK RICE WITH 1 TEASPOON SALT IN BOILING WATER UNTIL TENDER. DRAIN WELL AND KEEP HOT. COMBINE MAYONNAISE, ONION, 1/2 TEASPOON SALT AND PEPPER. ADD HAM, CHEESE, PICKLE AND HOT RICE. TOSS IN PEAS LIGHTLY WITH A FORK. REFRIGERATE FOR A SHORT TIME (BEST IF NOT TOO COLD). SERVE ON LETTUCE AND GARNISH WITH TOMATO WEDGES.

PECAN-PINEAPPLE ICE BOX DESSERT

1 CUP SUGAR
1/2 LB. BUTTER (OR MARG.)
2 EGG YOLKS
1 - 14-OUNCE CAN DRAINED, CRUSHED PINEAPPLE
1 CUP CHOPPED PECANS
1 LB. OR LESS VANILLA WAFERS, CRUSHED

CREAM BUTTER AND SUGAR 'TIL FLUFFY. ADD EGG YOLKS ONE AT A TIME AND BEAT WELL WITH ELECTRIC MIXER. ADD DRAINED PINEAPPLE AND PECANS. LAYER ALTERNATELY IN 9 x 9 PAN, CRUSHED VANILLA WAFERS AND PINEAPPLE MIXTURE. REFRIGERATE, COVERED, OVERNIGHT. SLICE IN SQUARES AND TOP WITH WHIPPED CREAM OR DREAM WHIP. SERVES 12.

FRIED CHICKEN THIGHS

SAUERKRAUT SOUFFLÉ

CELERY AND CARROT STICKS

PEARS ROSÉ

SAUERKRAUT SOUFFLÉ

THIS IS DELECTABLE AND DIFFERENT. IF YOU HAVE A GUEST WHO DOESN'T LIKE SAUERKRAUT, DON'T TELL HER WHAT'S IN THE SOUFFLÉ - SHE'LL NEVER GUESS!

3 TABLESPOONS BUTTER	1/8 TEASPOON PEPPER
1 TEASPOON CORN STARCH	1 CUP CHOPPED FINE SAUERKRAUT
1 CUP MILK	2 TABLESPOONS CHOPPED PARSLEY
3 BEATEN EGG YOLKS	3 EGG WHITES, BEATEN 'TIL STIFF
1/4 TEASPOON SALT	FINE BREAD CRUMBS

MELT BUTTER IN TOP OF A DOUBLE BOILER; ADD CORN STARCH AND BLEND; BLEND IN MILK. COOK UNTIL THICKENED. ADD EGG YOLKS, BLEND, AND COOK 2 MINUTES. ADD SEASONINGS. ADD THE CHOPPED SAUERKRAUT AND CHOPPED PARSLEY. BLEND ALL TOGETHER. FOLD IN THE BEATEN EGG WHITES. POUR INTO A WELL-BUTTERED CASSEROLE AND TOP WITH FINE BREAD CRUMBS. BAKE AT 350 DEGREES FOR 30 MINUTES. SERVES 6.

PEARS ROSÉ

20-OUNCE CAN PEAR HALVES
1/4 CUP SUGAR
2 TABLESPOONS GRATED ORANGE RIND
3-INCH CINNAMON STICK
1 TABLESPOON FRESH LEMON JUICE
1/2 CUP STILL ROSÉ WINE

DRAIN PEARS, RESERVE SYRUP. COMBINE SYRUP, SUGAR, ORANGE RIND AND CINNAMON STICK IN SMALL SAUCEPAN. BRING TO BOIL AND CONTINUE BOILING UNTIL LIQUID IS REDUCED TO 1/2 CUP. REMOVE FROM HEAT. COOL. BLEND LEMON JUICE AND ROSÉ WINE INTO COOLED SYRUP. POUR OVER PEARS. CHILL THOROUGHLY IN REFRIGERATOR BEFORE SERVING.

* * * * * *

SPARKLING ORANGE JUICE

CHICKEN CRÊPES

FROSTED PEARS WITH FRUIT SAUCE

SPARKLING ORANGE JUICE

THIS CAN BE MADE FOR ANY NUMBER OF GUESTS. SIMPLY MIX TOGETHER ONE-HALF OF WHATEVER QUANTITY YOU WANT TO MAKE OF ORANGE JUICE - THE OTHER HALF, SPARKLING WHITE WINE. VERY SIMPLE!

CHICKEN CRÊPES

CRÊPES MAKE AN ELEGANT LUNCHEON. WE SOMETIMES SPLURGE AND HAVE LUNCH AT A NEARBY FRENCH CRÊPE RESTAURANT, AND OCCASIONALLY GO ALL OUT AND END UP WITH THEIR FABULOUS CHOCOLATE CRÊPES. THIS RECIPE IS MARILYN'S AND IT'S SO MOUTH-WATERING. YOU COULD SERVE THEM TO THE QUEEN. THEY'D CERTAINLY GET ROYAL APPROVAL.

1/4 CUP MARGARINE

2 TABLESPOONS FINELY CHOPPED ONION

2 TABLESPOONS FINELY CHOPPED CELERY

1/4 CUP FLOUR

3/4 CUP MILK

1 CUP CHICKEN STOCK

1/4 CUP DRY WHITE WINE, OR

1/4 CUP MORE STOCK

1/2 TEASPOON SALT

PEPPER

1/4 CUP MILK

1 EGG YOLK

2 CUPS CHOPPED, COOKED CHICKEN

1/2 CUP CHOPPED, COOKED OR CANNED MUSHROOMS

(2 TABLESPOONS FINELY CHOPPED PIMENTO

(1/4 CUP FINELY CHOPPED GREEN PEPPER

OR

2 TABLESPOONS DRIED PEPPER FLAKES SOAKED IN A LITTLE HOT WATER AND DRAINED

CHICKEN CRÊPES - continued

MELT BUTTER IN SAUCEPAN. ADD ONION AND CELERY AND COOK 'TIL TENDER - NOT BROWN. SPRINKLE IN AND BLEND FLOUR. REMOVE FROM HEAT AND ADD 3/4 CUP MILK, STOCK, WINE, SALT AND PEPPER. BLEND. COOK, STIRRING WELL, UNTIL BOILING, THICKENED AND SMOOTH. BEAT 1/4 CUP MILK AND EGG YOLK TOGETHER. STIR IN A LITTLE OF HOT MIXTURE AND THEN STIR BACK INTO HOT SAUCE. REMOVE FROM HEAT AND MEASURE OUT 1 CUP OF SAUCE AND SET ASIDE.

HEAT BROILER - LEAVE RACK IN MIDDLE OF OVEN. STIR CHICKEN, MUSHROOMS, PIMENTO AND GREEN PEPPER INTO SAUCE REMAINING IN SAUCEPAN. TOP EACH OF 12 CRÊPES WITH ABOUT 1/4 CUP CHICKEN MIXTURE. FOLD IN SIDES OF CRÊPES AND ROLL. PUT CLOSE TOGETHER IN A BUTTERED BAKING DISH ABOUT 12" x 8" x 1-1/2". (I LIKE TO HAVE MY BAKING DISH PREHEATED). SPOON RESERVED SAUCE OVER CRÊPES AND SPRINKLE WITH PAPRIKA. BROIL LOW UNDER BROILER (MIDDLE OF OVEN) UNTIL HEATED THROUGH AND SAUCE IS BUBBLING. IF YOU ARE PREPARING AHEAD AND CHILLING, COVER CRÊPES AND BAKE IN PREHEATED OVEN AT 375 DEGREES UNTIL HEATED, ABOUT 30 MINUTES. THEN REMOVE COVER AND BROIL LOW UNDER BROILER FOR A FEW MINUTES UNTIL BUBBLY.

N.B. NICE WITH A GRATING OF SWISS CHEESE OVER TOP BEFORE BROILING. SERVES 6.

CHICKEN CRÊPES - continued

CRÊPES: (20 - 24 CRÊPES)

4 EGGS

1/2 TEASPOON SALT

1-1/4 CUPS SIFTED ALL-PURPOSE FLOUR

1-3/4 CUPS MILK

1/4 CUP BUTTER OR MARGARINE, MELTED AND COOLED TO LUKEWARM

BEAT EGGS AND SALT. ADD REMAINING INGREDIENTS AND BEAT SMOOTH. LET STAND AT LEAST 1 HOUR. PUT ABOUT 2 TABLESPOONS BATTER ON LIGHTLY GREASED GRIDDLE AND SPREAD AS THINLY AS POSSIBLE TO MAKE A PANCAKE ABOUT 5" TO 6" IN DIAMETER. BROWN FIRST SIDE WELL. TURN. COOK JUST LONG ENOUGH TO SET SECOND SIDE. WELL BROWNED SIDE SHOULD BE TO OUTSIDE OF ROLLED CRÊPE.

ANY LEFTOVER CRÊPES MAY BE STORED IN FREEZER WITH WAXED PAPER BETWEEN AND WRAPPED IN FOIL AND USED AT A LATER DATE WITH ANY FILLING.

FROSTED PEARS WITH FRUIT SAUCE

4 PEAR HALVES (CANNED OR VERY-RIPE FRESH, PEELED)

4 SCOOPS PINEAPPLE SHERBET

1/2 CUP BERRY-FLAVOURED SYRUP

2 TABLESPOONS RUM (OPTIONAL)

PLACE PEAR HALVES IN SHERBET DISHES. TOP WITH SHERBET. MIX SYRUP AND RUM AND POUR OVER DESSERTS. (FOR SYRUP, USE BLACKBERRY, ELDERBERRY, BLUEBERRY OR RED RASPBERRY).

YOU CAN HAVE THIS ELEGANT BUT EASY SUMMER LUNCHEON WITH A MINIMUM OF FUSS. UNLIKE ME (WHO IS USUALLY TEARING AROUND SETTING THE TABLE, DUSTING THE FURNITURE OR HAVE MY HEAD STUCK IN THE OVEN TESTING THE SOUFFLÉ), YOU CAN BE STRETCHED OUT ON A SUN LOUNGE ON THE PATIO OR GLUED TO THE TV WATCHING YOUR FAVOURITE SOAP OPERA.

TOMATO BOUILLON

SALMON MOUSSE

WITH

CUCUMBER DILL SAUCE

MONKEY BREAD

PEACH DELIGHT

TOMATO BOUILLON

2 CUPS TOMATO JUICE

1 - 10-1/2 OZ. CAN CONDENSED BEEF BROTH

1/2 TABLESPOON LEMON JUICE

1/4 TEASPOON WORCESTERSHIRE SAUCE

1/4 TEASPOON HORSERADISH

1/4 CUP SHERRY (OPTIONAL)

MEASURE ALL INGREDIENTS EXCEPT WINE INTO SAUCEPAN. HEAT SLOWLY FOR 30 MINUTES, STIRRING OCCASIONALLY. JUST BEFORE SERVING, STIR IN WINE. ABOUT 7 - 1/2 CUP SERVINGS.

SALMON MOUSSE WITH DILL SAUCE

ONE OF MY FAVOURITE "MAKE-THE-DAY BEFORE" RECIPES.

- 2 TABLESPOONS PLUS 1 TEASPOON FLOUR
- 2 TABLESPOONS PLUS 1 TEASPOON SUGAR
- 1-1/2 TEASPOONS PREPARED MUSTARD (DIJON, IF AVAILABLE)
- 1-1/2 TEASPOONS SALT
- DASH CAYENNE PEPPER
- 3 EGGS
- 1-1/8 CUPS MILK (1 CUP PLUS 2 TABLESPOONS)
- 6 TABLESPOONS TARRAGON VINEGAR
- 2 TABLESPOONS PLUS 1 TEASPOON BUTTER
- 1-1/2 TABLESPOONS PLAIN GELATIN
- 1/4 CUP COLD WATER
- 2 - 7-1/4 OUNCE CANS RED SALMON - FLAKED
- 3/4 CUP WHIPPING CREAM - WHIPPED

SOFTEN GELATIN IN COLD WATER. IN TOP OF DOUBLE BOILER, COMBINE FLOUR AND SUGAR. MIX WELL. ADD MUSTARD, SALT, CAYENNE AND EGGS. WHISK UNTIL WELL COMBINED. WHISK IN MILK. STIR SMOOTH. SLOWLY ADD THE VINEGAR TO AVOID CURDLING. COOK, STIRRING CONSTANTLY, OVER HOT WATER 'TIL THICK AND SMOOTH. REMOVE FROM HEAT AND STIR IN BUTTER. ADD GELATIN AND STIR UNTIL DISSOLVED. FOLD IN FLAKED SALMON. CHILL UNTIL IT BEGINS TO SET. FOLD IN WHIPPED CREAM. POUR INTO OILED, 5-CUP MOLD. CHILL UNTIL FIRM. SERVES 8.

DILL SAUCE:

- 1 SMALL CUCUMBER, PEELED, SEEDED AND COARSELY GRATED
- SALT
- 3/4 CUP SOUR CREAM
- SCANT TABLESPOON LEMON JUICE
- 3/4 TEASPOON DILL WEED
- 3/4 TEASPOON CHOPPED CHIVES

SPRINKLE CUCUMBER WITH SALT. LET STAND FOR 1 HOUR AND DRAIN WELL. COMBINE WITH ALL OTHER INGREDIENTS AND CHILL SEVERAL HOURS. STIR BEFORE SERVING.

MONKEY BREAD

IF YOUR GUESTS ARE AT ALL CALORIE-CONSCIOUS, THEY'LL HATE YOU FOR SERVING THIS BREAD. ONE "DIAMOND" TASTES LIKE MORE!

- 2 PACKAGES DRY YEAST
- 1 TEASPOON SUGAR
- 1/4 CUP WARM WATER (110-115 DEG.)
- 1/2 CUP BUTTER
- 1/3 CUP SUGAR
- 1 TEASPOON SALT
- 3/4 CUP SCALDED MILK
- 5 CUPS FLOUR
- 3 LARGE EGGS
- 1/2 LB. OR MORE MELTED BUTTER FOR DIPPING

MONKEY BREAD - continued

DISSOLVE YEAST AND 1 TEASPOON SUGAR IN WARM WATER. COMBINE BUTTER, 1/3 CUP SUGAR AND SALT; ADD SCALDED MILK. STIR TO MELT BUTTER. COOL. ADD YEAST, HALF THE FLOUR AND EGGS. BEAT THOROUGHLY. STIR IN REST OF FLOUR TO MAKE A SOFT, BUT NOT STICKY, DOUGH. TURN OUT ONTO A FLOURED BREAD-BOARD; KNEAD UNTIL SMOOTH AND SATINY - 8 TO 10 MINUTES. PLACE IN A BUTTERED BOWL; COVER AND LET RISE IN WARM PLACE FREE FROM DRAFTS UNTIL DOUBLED IN BULK. PUNCH DOWN; TURN OUT ONTO A FLOURED BOARD. ROLL OUT 1/4" THICK. CUT DOUGH INTO DIAMONDS, OR ANY SHAPE PREFERRED. DIP EACH PIECE INTO MELTED BUTTER; ARRANGE IN A BUTTERED 10" TUBE PAN. COVER AND LET RISE AGAIN UNTIL ALMOST DOUBLED IN BULK. BAKE AT 375 DEGREES FOR 45 MINUTES OR UNTIL BROWNED AND DONE. SERVE WARM. GUESTS JUST PULL OFF THE BUTTERY, DELICIOUS DIAMONDS.

HEAVENLY PEACHES

THIS ONLY TAKES 10 MINUTES TO THROW TOGETHER, BUT IT'S DIFFERENT - AND GOOD! I EVEN MAKE MY OWN PEANUT BRITTLE BUT, OF COURSE, YOU CAN BUY THIS. HOWEVER, THE NEIGHBOURHOOD CHILDREN LOVE THE LEFT-OVER CANDY - AND SO DOES RUTH!

HEAVENLY PEACHES - continued

4 LARGE PEACH HALVES, FRESH OR CANNED
1/2 CUP HEAVY CREAM, WHIPPED
1/2 CUP PEANUT BRITTLE, CRUSHED

TOP EACH HALF OF A PEACH WITH WHIPPED CREAM. SPRINKLE PEANUT BRITTLE ON TOP. DOUBLE THIS RECIPE FOR 8 GUESTS.

PEANUT BRITTLE:

2 CUPS WHITE SUGAR	1 CUP BUTTER
1 CUP CORN SYRUP	2 CUPS RAW PEANUTS
1/2 CUP WATER	1 TEASPOON BAKING SODA

IN 3-QUART PAN, HEAT TOGETHER SYRUP, SUGAR AND WATER, STIRRING UNTIL SUGAR DISSOLVES. WHEN SYRUP BOILS, BLEND IN BUTTER. STIR FREQUENTLY AFTER TEMPERATURE REACHES 230 DEGREES. ADD PEANUTS WHEN TEMPERATURE REACHES 280 DEGREES. STIR CONSTANTLY TO HARD CRACK STAGE (305 DEGREES). REMOVE FROM HEAT, QUICKLY STIR IN SODA, MIXING WELL. POUR ONTO TWO BUTTERED COOKIE SHEETS. LOOSEN FROM PAN WHEN CANDY HARDENS. BREAK INTO PIECES. MAKES 2-1/2 POUNDS. LOTS LEFT OVER FOR MUNCHING!

MOLDED SLAW SALAD

FRENCH HAM ROLLS

APPLE PUDDING WITH CITRUS SAUCE

MOLDED SLAW SALAD

I TOOK THIS TO A POTLUCK SUPPER AND TRIED TO LOOK BLASÉ WHEN THE COMPLIMENTS WERE BEING THROWN AROUND!

- 2 - 3-OUNCE PACKAGES LEMON GELATIN
- 2 CUPS BOILING WATER
- 1/2 CUP DILL PICKLE JUICE
- 1/4 CUP COLD WATER
- 2 TABLESPOONS FINELY CHOPPED ONION
- 2 TABLESPOONS LEMON JUICE
- 1/2 TEASPOON SALT
- 1 CUP MAYONNAISE
- 2-1/2 CUPS CHOPPED CABBAGE
- 1/2 CUP SHREDDED CARROT
- 1/2 CUP CHOPPED, SEEDED, PEELED CUCUMBER
- 1/3 CUP CHOPPED DILL PICKLE
- LEAF LETTUCE
- CARROT STICKS, RADISHES, PICKLES OR OLIVES

OIL A 6-CUP RING MOLD AND SET ASIDE. IN A LARGE BOWL, DISSOLVE GELATIN IN 2 CUPS BOILING WATER. STIR IN DILL PICKLE JUICE, 1/4 CUP COLD WATER, ONION, LEMON JUICE AND SALT; MIX WELL. ADD MAYONNAISE AND BEAT WITH A WHISK UNTIL SMOOTH. REFRIGERATE UNTIL PARTLY SET. FOLD IN CABBAGE, CARROT, CUCUMBER AND DILL PICKLE. POUR MIXTURE INTO THE OILED MOLD. REFRIGERATE 6 HOURS OR OVERNIGHT 'TIL SET. UNMOLD ON PLATTER AND FILL CENTER OF MOLD WITH ASSORTED RELISHES. SERVES ABOUT 12. GOOD FOR CHURCH SUPPERS.

FRENCH HAM ROLLS

8-OUNCE PACKAGE REFRIGERATED CRESCENT ROLLS

MELTED BUTTER

4 THIN SLICES COOKED HAM (THE RECTANGULAR SLICES YOU BUY FOR SANDWICHES)

PREPARED MUSTARD

1/4 CUP GRATED PARMESAN CHEESE

2 TABLESPOONS CHOPPED PARSLEY

SEPARATE REFRIGERATED BISCUITS AS DIRECTED ON PACKAGE. (DO YOU EVER HAVE TROUBLE SEPARATING PACKAGED ROLLS OR BISCUITS? I DO - AND END UP TRYING TO PASTE THEM TOGETHER!) BRUSH WITH MELTED BUTTER. CUT HAM DIAGONALLY TO FORM 8 TRIANGLES. LAY ONE TRIANGLE OF HAM ON EACH BISCUIT, TRIMMING, IF NECESSARY. SPREAD WITH MUSTARD. COMBINE CHEESE AND PARSLEY AND SPRINKLE SOME ON EACH OF EIGHT ROLLS. ROLL UP FROM WIDE END TO POINT. PLACE ON LIGHTLY GREASED COOKIE SHEET, POINTS DOWN. TURN ENDS TO FORM CRESCENT. BAKE ABOUT 13 MINUTES AT 375 DEGREES UNTIL GOLDEN.

APPLE PUDDING WITH CITRUS SAUCE

1/4 CUP BUTTER	1/2 TEASPOON CINNAMON
3/4 CUP SUGAR	1/4 TEASPOON SALT
1 EGG	1/4 TEASPOON NUTMEG
1 CUP + 2 TABLESPOONS FLOUR	1-1/2 CUPS COARSELY GRATED, PEELED AND CORED APPLES
1 TEASPOON BAKING SODA	1 TABLESPOON CREAM

IN A LARGE BOWL CREAM TOGETHER THE SUGAR AND BUTTER (SOFTENED), AND BEAT IN THE EGG. INTO ANOTHER BOWL SIFT TOGETHER THE FLOUR, BAKING SODA, CINNAMON, SALT AND NUTMEG. ADD THE FLOUR MIXTURE TO THE SUGAR MIXTURE AND STIR IN THE APPLES AND THE CREAM. PUT THE MIXTURE IN A BUTTERED, 1-QUART BAKING DISH AND BAKE IN A 350-DEGREE OVEN FOR 45 TO 50 MINUTES, OR UNTIL IT IS JUST SET. SERVE THE PUDDING WITH CITRUS SAUCE.

CITRUS SAUCE:

1 CUP BOILING WATER	1 CUP ORANGE JUICE
1/3 CUP SUGAR	2 TABLESPOONS SOFTENED BUTTER
2 TABLESPOONS CORNSTARCH	ORANGE LIQUEUR TO TASTE (OPTIONAL)

COMBINE SUGAR AND CORNSTARCH IN SAUCEPAN, STIR IN BOILING WATER AND RETURN TO A BOIL, STIRRING CONSTANTLY, THEN SIMMER FOR 5 MINUTES. STIR IN ORANGE JUICE, BUTTER AND, IF DESIRED, THE ORANGE LIQUEUR. MAKES ABOUT 2 CUPS.

BAKED TOMATOES

HOT SALMON SOUFFLÉ

KATHY'S HERB BREAD

BRANDIED GRAPES

BAKED TOMATOES

3 RIPE, MEDIUM TOMATOES

3/4 TEASPOON PREPARED MUSTARD

1 TABLESPOON MINCED ONION

1-1/2 TEASPOONS WORCESTERSHIRE SAUCE

SALT

3 TABLESPOONS SOFT, BUTTERED BREAD CRUMBS

HEAT OVEN TO 375 DEGREES. REMOVE STEM END OF TOMATOES AND CUT IN HALF CROSSWISE. ARRANGE CUT SIDE UP IN BAKING DISH. SPREAD WITH MUSTARD, SPRINKLE WITH ONION AND WORCESTERSHIRE SAUCE. SALT LIGHTLY AND TOP WITH CRUMBS. BAKE 25 TO 30 MINUTES UNTIL HEATED THROUGH BUT STILL HOLDING THEIR SHAPE. SERVES 6.

SALMON SOUFFLÉ

2 TABLESPOONS MELTED BUTTER

2 TABLESPOONS FLOUR

1 CUP MILK

2 EGG YOLKS

1/2 TEASPOON SALT

1/4 TEASPOON NUTMEG

SPECK PEPPER

1# CAN SALMON (RED) FLAKED

2 EGG WHITES BEATEN STIFF

LEMON WEDGES

MELT BUTTER OVER DOUBLE BOILER, STIR IN FLOUR AND SLOWLY ADD MILK. COOK OVER HOT WATER UNTIL SMOOTH AND THICK. BEAT YOLKS AND SLOWLY STIR INTO SAUCE. ADD SALT, NUTMEG AND PEPPER. FOLD IN SKINNED, FLAKED SALMON, THEN EGG WHITES BEATEN STIFF. TURN INTO GREASED, 1-1/2-QUART SOUFFLÉ DISH AND BAKE AT 350 DEGREES FOR 45 MINUTES. SERVE WITH LEMON WEDGES TO 4.

KATHY'S HERB BREAD

ANOTHER "STEAL" FROM "WITH A PINCH OF PINE CONES AND CHIPMUNKS" - BUT IT FITS IN SO WELL WITH NEARLY EVERY MENU AND IS THE EASIEST BREAD RECIPE TO MAKE. IF YOU'VE NEVER TRIED IT BEFORE, NOW'S THE TIME. YOU'LL LIKE IT!

1 LOAF FRENCH BREAD (SMALL LOAF)

MIX TOGETHER:
- 1 STICK MARGARINE (1/2 CUP) SOFTENED
- 1 TABLESPOON DRIED PARSLEY
- 1 TABLESPOON MINCED ONION (OR DRIED ONION, OR FROZEN)
- 1/2 TABLESPOON BASIL
- LITTLE SUMMER SAVORY
- 2 TABLESPOONS LEMON JUICE

SLICE BREAD IN THIN SLICES AND SPREAD ABOVE MIXTURE ON BOTH SIDES (SPREAD THIN). PUT LOAF TOGETHER AND WRAP IN FOIL. PUT IN 350-DEGREE OVEN UNTIL IT IS HEATED THROUGH. (I USUALLY LEAVE IT IN FOR 20 MINUTES). I SOMETIMES SPREAD THE MIXTURE A LITTLE THICKER, AND JUST ON ONE SIDE.

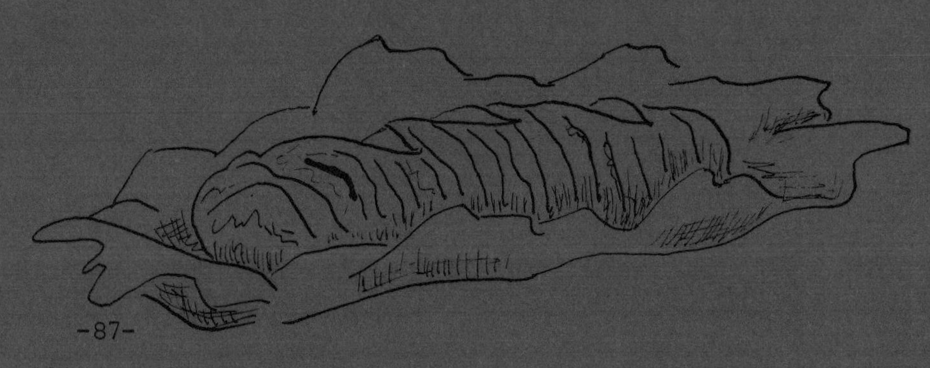

BRANDIED GRAPES

THIS IS SO VERY EASY TO MAKE - AND SO DELICIOUS!

2 POUNDS CALIFORNIA GRAPES
(PREFERABLY SEEDLESS)

BROWN SUGAR

1 CUP SOUR CREAM

1/2 CUP HEAVY CREAM

1/2 POUND CONFECTIONERS' SUGAR

1/4 CUP BRANDY

SPRINKLE GRAPES WITH BROWN SUGAR. COMBINE SOUR CREAM, HEAVY CREAM AND CONFECTIONERS' SUGAR. MIX THE CREAM MIXTURE AND BRANDY TOGETHER WITH THE GRAPES. PUT IN FREEZER COMPARTMENT FOR 10 - 15 MINUTES. SERVE IMMEDIATELY.

HOT CRAB SOUFFLÉ

FRESH ASPARAGUS TIPS

LEMON PUDDING

TRY THIS MENU ON SPECIAL LUNCHEON GUESTS SOME SUNNY, APRIL NOON-HOUR! THE SOUFFLÉ, WHILE A BIT COSTLY, IS IMPRESSIVE, THE FRESH ASPARAGUS IS A BREATH OF SPRING AND THE LEMON PUDDING IS JUST THE LIGHT TOUCH NEEDED AT THE END OF THE MEAL. YOU'RE SURE TO SCORE A GRAND SLAM WITH THIS MENU.

HOT CRAB SOUFFLÉ

PREPARE THE NIGHT BEFORE - MY FAVOURITE KIND OF RECIPE!

8 - 10 SLICES WHITE BREAD, DICED
2 CUPS CRAB (OR SHRIMP)
1 CUP MAYONNAISE
1 SMALL ONION, CHOPPED
1 CUP CELERY, CHOPPED
1 MEDIUM PEPPER, CHOPPED
1 TEASPOON MINCED PARSLEY
1 TEASPOON GRATED LEMON PEEL
1 TEASPOON SALT
1/4 TEASPOON PEPPER
4 EGGS
3 CUPS MILK
1 CUP MUSHROOM SOUP UNDILUTED
GRATED PARMESAN CHEESE

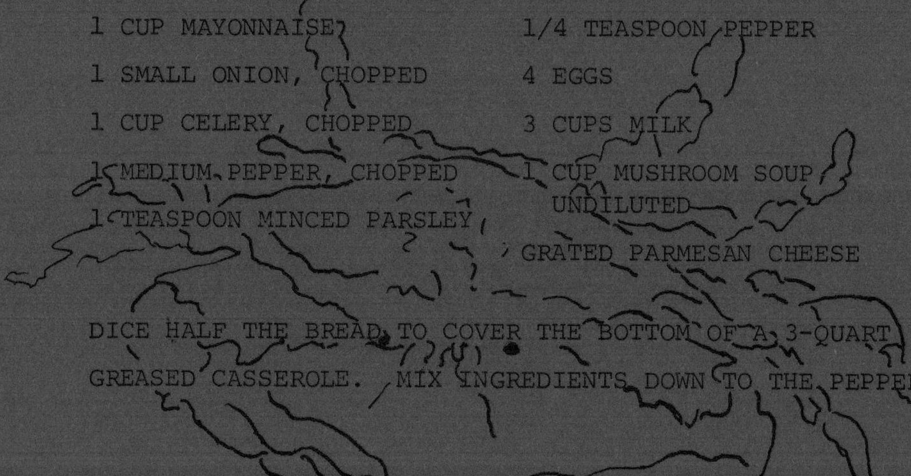

DICE HALF THE BREAD TO COVER THE BOTTOM OF A 3-QUART GREASED CASSEROLE. MIX INGREDIENTS DOWN TO THE PEPPER,

HOT CRAB SOUFFLÉ - continued

ARRANGE OVER BREAD, THEN COVER WITH THE REST OF THE DICED BREAD. BEAT EGGS AND MILK, POUR OVER, COVER AND REFRIGERATE OVERNIGHT. BAKE UNCOVERED AT 325 DEGREES FOR 1 HOUR, 15 MINUTES. COVER WITH SOUP AND CHEESE, THEN PUT UNDER BROILER FOR 2 MINUTES.
SERVES 12 - SO IT'S NOT REALLY ALL THAT EXTRAVAGANT!

LEMON PUDDING

3/4 CUP GRAHAM WAFER CRUMBS
1 CUP WHIPPING CREAM
3 EGGS
1 CUP SUGAR
1 LEMON
1 ORANGE
1 PACKAGE UNFLAVOURED GELATIN

LINE A 9 x 5 LOAF PAN WITH 1/2 CUP GRAHAM WAFER CRUMBS. IN A SMALL BOWL, ADD GELATIN TO JUICE OF LEMON AND ORANGE. SET IN A LARGER BOWL OF HOT WATER TO KEEP THE GELATIN MIXTURE LIQUID. BEAT EGG WHITES UNTIL STIFF. GRADUALLY, ADD 1/2 CUP SUGAR, CONTINUE TO BEAT. WHIP CREAM UNTIL STIFF. BEAT EGG YOLKS IN A LARGE BOWL WITH 1/2 CUP SUGAR UNTIL LEMON COLOURED. (BY THIS TIME, I HAVE EVERY BOWL IN THE HOUSE ON THE COUNTER!) ADD LEMON AND ORANGE MIXTURE TO YOLKS. FOLD IN EGG WHITES. FOLD IN WHIPPED CREAM. POUR

INTO LOAF PAN AND SPRINKLE WITH REMAINING GRAHAM WAFER CRUMBS. FREEZE FOR 1/2 DAY BEFORE SERVING. IT DOESN'T HURT IT TO STAY LONGER IN THE FREEZER. ONE HOUR BEFORE SERVING, REMOVE FROM PAN ONTO SERVING PLATE AND LEAVE IN THE REFRIGERATOR UNTIL IT'S TIME TO SERVE.

OLD-FASHIONED, BUT TERRIFIC!

* * * * *

HERE'S A NICE, EASY, BRIDGE LUNCHEON. GOOD AT ANY TIME OF THE YEAR.

MUSHROOM ROLLS

ASSORTED PICKLES - RADISH-ROSES - CELERY STICKS

BAKED FRUIT COMPOTE WITH ICE CREAM

* * * * *

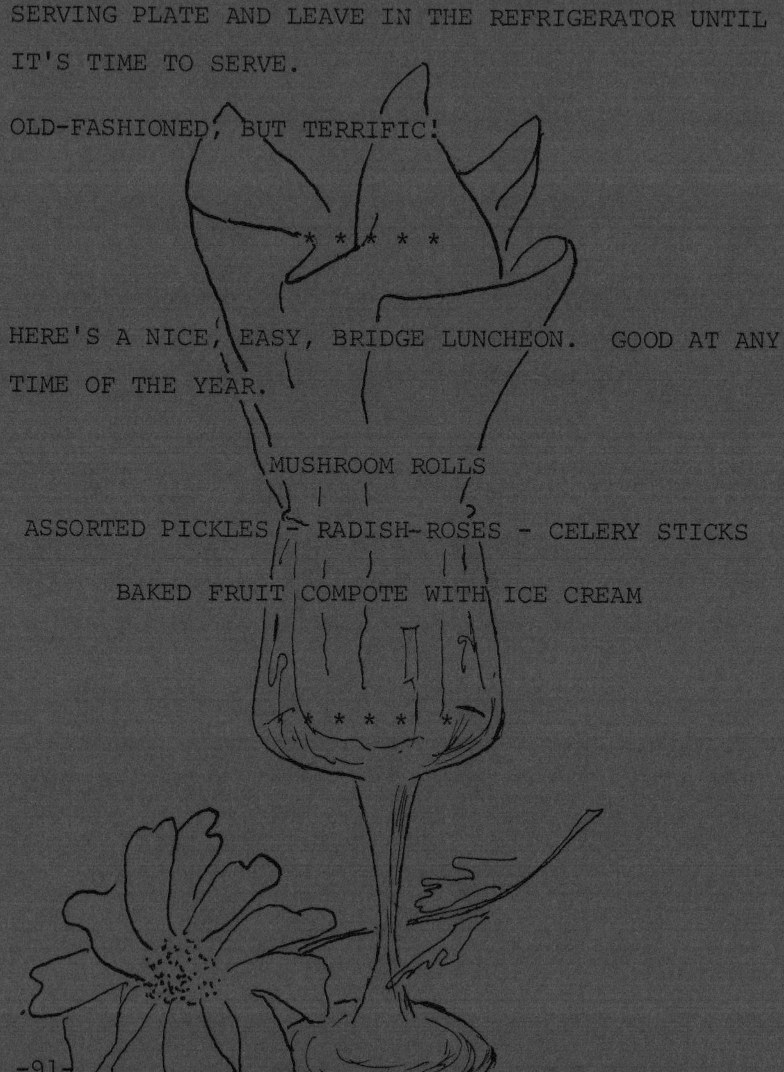

MUSHROOM ROLLS

1 LOAF THIN-SLICED BREAD, TRIMMED

1/2 POUND FRESH MUSHROOMS, CHOPPED

1/2 CUP BUTTER

3 TABLESPOONS FLOUR

1 CUP LIGHT CREAM

3/4 TEASPOON SALT

1/4 TEASPOON MSG (ACCENT)

2 TEASPOONS CHIVES

1 TEASPOON LEMON JUICE

BUTTER, SOFTENED

ROLL BREAD SLICES THIN AND FLAT. SAUTÉ MUSHROOMS IN BUTTER FOR 5 MINUTES. BLEND IN FLOUR AND STIR IN CREAM. COOK, STIRRING CONSTANTLY, UNTIL THICKENED. STIR IN SALT, MSG, CHIVES AND LEMON JUICE. REMOVE FROM HEAT. PLACE 1 TO 2 TEASPOONS OF THE MIXTURE ON EACH SLICE OF BREAD. ROLL. BUTTER THE TOP SIDE OF EACH. FREEZE. WHEN READY TO SERVE, CUT IN HALF AND PLACE ON BAKING SHEET. BAKE AT 400 DEGREES FOR ABOUT 10 MINUTES OR UNTIL GOLDEN. EIGHT SERVINGS.

BAKED FRUIT COMPOTE WITH ICE CREAM

1 - 10-OUNCE CAN EACH OF APRICOT HALVES AND PEARS

1 - 10-OUNCE CAN PLUMS, HALVED AND PITTED

1/2 CUP SYRUP DRAINED FROM FRUIT

1/2 CUP ORANGE MARMALADE

2 TEASPOONS GRATED LEMON RIND

VANILLA ICE CREAM

DRAIN FRUIT, RESERVING SYRUP. IF FRUIT HALVES ARE VERY LARGE, CUT INTO NICE CHUNKY SLICES. ARRANGE FRUIT IN SHALLOW BAKING DISH. COMBINE 1/2 CUP SYRUP, MARMALADE AND RIND AND BRING TO A BOIL. POUR OVER FRUIT AND BAKE AT 350 DEGREES FOR 15 TO 20 MINUTES. SERVE WARM OVER ICE CREAM.

CAN'T DAWDLE OVER THIS DESSERT - EAT IT BEFORE THE ICE CREAM MELTS!

CRESCENT ROLLS

TOMATO AND CHEESE ASPIC

TOSSED SALAD WITH WALNUTS AND

RED WINE DRESSING

NO-FAIL BABAS

COFFEE

THIS MENU CAN BE ADAPTED TO ANY NUMBER OF GUESTS. THE ASPIC IS A LARGE SALAD, JUST THROW A FEW EXTRA GREENS IN THE SALAD BOWL AND DOUBLE THE DESSERT RECIPE.

TOMATO AND CHEESE ASPIC

DELIGHTFULLY DIFFERENT - AND VERY TASTY!

2 CANS TOMATO SOUP

2-1/2 CUPS OF WATER

8-OUNCE PACKAGE CREAM CHEESE

1 ENVELOPE UNFLAVOURED GELATIN

1 LARGE LEMON JELLO

1 CUP SALAD DRESSING

1 CUP FINELY CHOPPED CELERY

1/3 CUP FINELY CHOPPED GREEN ONION

2/3 CUP FINELY CHOPPED GREEN PEPPER

TOMATO AND CHEESE ASPIC - continued

DISSOLVE GELATIN IN 1/2 CUP COLD WATER. HEAT REMAINING LIQUID (WATER AND SOUP), DISSOLVE JELLO AND GELATIN IN HOT MIXTURE. ADD CHEESE, STIR UNTIL WELL DISSOLVED. WHIP SLOWLY WITH BEATER TO BLEND COMPLETELY. ALLOW TO COOL. THEN MIX IN SALAD DRESSING UNTIL WELL BLENDED. LET PARTIALLY SET AND ADD SOLIDS. ALLOW TO GEL. MAKE THE DAY BEFORE. SERVES 12.

TOSSED SALAD WITH WALNUTS AND RED WINE DRESSING

EMPTY YOUR CRISPER AND TOSS TOGETHER EVERYTHING THAT'S GREEN - LETTUCE, ENDIVE, SPINACH, PARSLEY. ADD WALNUTS TOASTED IN BUTTER MIXED WITH A BIT OF GARLIC SALT.

RED WINE DRESSING:

1/2 CUP RED WINE VINEGAR
1/2 CUP SALAD OIL
1 TABLESPOON PREPARED MUSTARD

NO-FAIL BABAS

THIS RECIPE IS JULIE'S, A CONNOISEUR OF FOOD WHO LIKES TO DINE IN ELEGANT FRENCH RESTAURANTS.

1 - 14-OUNCE CAN APRICOT HALVES (OR PEACHES)

3/4 CUP LIQUID HONEY

1/2 CUP FRESH ORANGE JUICE

3 TABLESPOONS OF RUM (OR 3 TABLESPOONS WATER AND 1 TEASPOON RUM FLAVORING)

6 INDIVIDUAL SPONGE CAKE SHELLS

VANILLA ICE CREAM

SLICED ALMONDS, TOASTED

DRAIN APRICOTS (OR PEACHES), RESERVING SYRUP. COMBINE SYRUP, HONEY AND ORANGE JUICE; SIMMER 15 MINUTES. ADD RUM (OR WATER AND RUM FLAVORING); RESERVE 3/4 CUP OF SAUCE. SPOON REMAINING SAUCE OVER CAKES. CHILL. BEFORE SERVING, TOP CAKES WITH FRUIT, ICE CREAM AND RESERVED SAUCE. SPRINKLE WITH ALMONDS. INSTEAD OF ALMONDS, TOASTED COCONUT CAN BE USED.

SERVES 6.

HOT CUCUMBER SOUP

LIME SALAD SUPREME

HERB ROLLS

DEEP FRIED ICE CREAM

EVERYONE WHO HAS TRIED THE HERB ROLLS FROM "WITH A PINCH OF PINE CONES AND CHIPMUNKS" RAVES ABOUT THEM, BUT IT IS ALSO SAID THEY'RE HABIT FORMING; YOU JUST CAN'T STOP EATING THEM. ANYWAY, HERE'S THE RECIPE AGAIN. TRY THEM (SO EASY!) - ALONG WITH THE HOT CUCUMBER SOUP, LIME SALAD SUPREME AND DEEP FRIED ICE CREAM. YOUR FRIENDS WILL BE IMPRESSED - AND YOU'LL END UP A LIFE MEMBER OF THE GOURMET COOKING LEAGUE!

HOT CUCUMBER SOUP

I BEGGED THIS RECIPE FROM TIBOR TAKACS, HEAD CHEF AT ASCONA PLACE, THAT FAMOUS GRAVENHURST, ONTARIO RESTAURANT. IT IS THE MOST DELICIOUS SOUP I HAVE EVER TASTED.

HOT CUCUMBER SOUP - continued

2 LARGE CUCUMBERS, PEELED AND SEEDED

2 OUNCES ONION

2 CUPS CHICKEN STOCK

2 CUPS MILK

1 CUP 35% CREAM (WHIPPING)

SALT AND PEPPER TO TASTE

1/8 TEASPOON THYME

DASH WORCESTERSHIRE SAUCE

1 OUNCE WHITE WINE (2 TABLESPOONS)

4 EGG YOLKS FOR LIAISON

PURÉE FIRST THREE INGREDIENTS IN BLENDER. BOIL WITH REMAINING INGREDIENTS EXCEPT CREAM, EGG YOLKS AND WINE. PREPARE A LIAISON OF THE CREAM AND EGG YOLKS. REMOVE SOUP FROM STOVE AND ADD SMALL AMOUNT TO LIAISON TO WARM. ADD LIAISON BACK TO SOUP AND ADD WHITE WINE. SERVE IMMEDIATELY. GARNISH WITH THIN SLICES OF CUCUMBER AND FRESHLY CHOPPED PARSLEY. DO NOT BOIL AFTER ADDITION OF LIAISON. SERVES 6.

LIME SALAD SUPREME

MARILYN MADE THIS FOR A CHURCH LUNCHEON, AND WAS IT EVER A HIT! I HAVE SINCE USED IT FOR A BRIDGE LUNCH, ALONG WITH THE HERB ROLLS, AND IT EVEN APPEALS TO THE CALORIE-CONSCIOUS.

2 - 3-OUNCE PACKAGES LIME GELATIN (OR LEMON)

2 CUPS BOILING WATER

1-1/2 CUPS COLD WATER

1 - 13-1/2 OUNCE CAN CRUSHED PINEAPPLE, DRAINED

2 BANANAS, DICED

1 CUP SMALL MARSHMALLOWS

2 TABLESPOONS BUTTER

1 TABLESPOON FLOUR

1 EGG, BEATEN

1/2 CUP SUGAR

1 CUP PINEAPPLE JUICE

1 CUP WHIPPING CREAM, WHIPP

1/2 CUP GRATED SWISS CHEESE

DISSOLVE GELATIN IN BOILING WATER. STIR IN COLD WATER AND LET STAND ABOUT 1/2 HOUR OR UNTIL SLIGHTLY SET. ADD PINEAPPLE, BANANAS AND MARSHMALLOWS. POUR INTO A 10-INCH SQUARE PAN. REFRIGERATE UNTIL FIRM. MELT BUTTER; ADD FLOUR AND EGG. STIR UNTIL SMOOTH. ADD SUGAR AND PINEAPPLE JUICE. COOK AND STIR UNTIL THICK. COOL. FOLD IN WHIPPED CREAM; POUR OVER TOP OF GELATIN. SPRINKLE WITH GRATED CHEESE AND REFRIGERATE. CUT IN SQUARES. MAKES 12 - 15 SERVINGS.

HERB ROLLS

1/4 CUP BUTTER OR MARGARINE
1-1/2 TEASPOONS PARSLEY FLAKES
1/2 TEASPOON DILL SEED
1/4 TEASPOON ONION FLAKES
1 PACKAGE REFRIGERATED BUTTERMILK BISCUITS

PUT THE BUTTER, PARSLEY, DILL SEED AND ONION FLAKES IN A 9" PIE PAN. LET MELT. BLEND WELL. CUT BISCUITS IN QUARTERS AND SWISH EACH ONE IN MELTED MIXTURE. ARRANGE PIECES TOUCHING IN THE PIE PAN. BAKE IN A 425-DEGREE OVEN FOR 12 MINUTES OR UNTIL GOLDEN BROWN. LET STAND A SHORT TIME TO ABSORB THE BUTTER AND HERBS. SERVES 6 - 8.

DEEP FRIED ICE CREAM

HERE'S ANOTHER ONE OF MR. TAKACS' EXCITING RECIPES. THIS IS THE MOST DELICIOUS, DELUXE DESSERT I'VE EVER TASTED, SO WAS THRILLED WHEN HE CONSENTED TO LET HIS SPECIAL RECIPE BE PUBLISHED. THIS WILL MAKE YOU THE LOCAL JULIA CHILD!

DEEP FRIED ICE CREAM - continued

1 SPONGE LAYER

6 SCOOPS VANILLA ICE CREAM

SAUCE:

3 OUNCES (3/4 CUP) BROWN SUGAR

3 OUNCES (1/4 CUP + 2 TABLESPOONS) WATER

2 OUNCES LEMON JUICE (1/4 CUP)

1 OUNCE DARK RUM (2 TABLESPOONS)

1/2 OUNCE (1 TABLESPOON) CORNSTARCH

BREADING PROCEDURE (2 EGG WHITES, FLOUR AND BREAD CRUMBS

CUT THIN (1/4 INCH) SLICES OF SPONGE CAKE. WRAP EACH ICE CREAM SCOOP COMPLETELY WITH CAKE SLICES. FREEZE. FOR SAUCE, BOIL TOGETHER SUGAR, WATER AND LEMON JUICE. COMBINE CORNSTARCH WITH A SMALL AMOUNT OF COLD WATER AND ADD UNTIL SAUCE REACHES DESIRED THICKNESS. REMOVE FROM STOVE AND ADD RUM. WORKING QUICKLY, JUST BEFORE SERVING, PUT ICE CREAM BALL THROUGH BREADING PROCEDURE: DREDGE BALLS WITH FLOUR, ROLL IN SLIGHTLY BEATEN (WITH FORK) EGG WHITES THEN IN FINE BREAD CRUMBS. DEEP FRY AT 325 DEGREES FOR ONE MINUTE. COVER WITH SAUCE AND SERVE IMMEDIATELY.

ADDITIONAL FAVOURITE RECIPES

ADDITIONAL FAVOURITE RECIPES

I N D E X

PAGE NO.

APPETIZERS

BEVERAGES

BREADS, BISCUITS AND MUFFINS

CAKES AND COOKIES

DESSERTS PAGE NO.

MAIN DISHES